Dear Stephe

with best wishes,

Murali

VIBRANT

TO HEAL AND BE WHOLE

From India to Oklahoma City

BY R. MURALI KRISHNA, M.D.

WITH KELLY DYER FRY

MCKINLEY BROWNE PUBLISHING

This book is dedicated to the following three angels
who helped shape me into the man I am today.

Thatha
You taught me how to see the power of the Unseen.

Amma
Your infinite love is felt by me every moment
and, through your suffering, you opened the window
of hope to many.

Sam
With your grace, your patience, and your heartfelt love,
you are a true divine gift for me.

CONTENTS

FOREWORD

When Terri White, Oklahoma's Commissioner of Mental
Health and Substance Abuse, told me she wanted me to meet
two friends of hers, I had no idea where it might lead. A dinner
was arranged in the home of Dr. Murali Krishna and his
wife, Sam. When I arrived, I was greeted with a big hug from
Murali. It was our first meeting, but didn't feel that way. I had
recently written an article about my son and his struggles with
addiction. The story ran on the front page of *The Oklahoman.*

He looked me in the eye and told me he loved every word. He
said he connected with me from the opening paragraph.

The evening was filled with great Indian food and great
conversation. Also attending was Reggie Whitten, a local
attorney who had lost his son to addiction. Murali asked us to
tell our stories about our sons. He then shared the story of the
struggles he had with his mother's illness.

Three souls clicked. We shared a common bond of pain.

Within a few weeks, I wrote a feature story on Murali for
The Oklahoman. I shared his experiences of joy and sorrow
interchanged with a few life lessons.

The holidays came and Murali invited me to lunch. For
those of you who know Murali and have been cast under his
motivational spell, you won't be surprised to learn that before
I finished my meal, he had talked me into helping him write a
book. How in the world did that happen? I have a full-time job
as editor of *The Oklahoman* and a very hectic schedule. Writing
a book has always been on my bucket list, but I thought it
would be in my retirement years, certainly not now.

But, Murali has a way of convincing you that all things are possible. I succumbed to his persistence and left the restaurant with enthusiasm and a handshake deal to help him with his memoir.

Every Thursday I dashed to his office around 4 p.m. for a one- to two-hour session. We both pledged to keep our standing appointment if at all possible. We rarely missed a Thursday from January through July.

Now it was time for the psychiatrist to sit in the hot seat. I asked question after question after question. Sometimes it was painful to see the sorrow in his eyes. And delightful when he suddenly recalled stories he had not thought about in years. He would laugh and say, "I'm not used to being asked the questions, I am used to asking the questions."

We decided to tackle his life story first. So, we wrote every other chapter. We saved the even chapters to discuss his life lessons. He has given countless speeches, so we pored through old presentations, notes and columns he had written.

I hope you enjoy reading the book as much as we did writing it. Murali is a wise man. In these pages, I hope you will learn to befriend him as he shares his stories.

And I hope you will take his lessons to heart.

Murali, Reggie, Terri and I continue to work on projects together. We stand shoulder to shoulder in effort to improve the lives of those suffering from mental illness and addiction.

No doubt, you will be hearing more from us.

– Kelly Dyer Fry

PREFACE

Throughout my many years of listening to patients, I have been awed by the resilience of the human spirit. Having experienced trauma as a child, I felt a special connectedness to my patients dealing with pain and suffering.

I have been driven my whole career to seek answers. We each come into this world as unique, spiritual beings. Life unfolds and brings with it many challenges. No life is shielded from pain. Sometimes the pain is physical, sometimes it is emotional. In both instances, our positive mental attitude and perseverance determine how we will not only survive, but thrive.

When we move through pain and live life more fully, we can become more than whole, we can become vibrant.

While thinking about a title for this book, I examined my own circumstances. Now in my sixties, I can truly say I have grown from pain in my life and have pushed myself to become vibrant. I have witnessed patients progress from healed to vibrant. I have seen Oklahoma City rise to vibrancy following the acts of terror on April 19, 1995.

My life has been blessed and I want to give back. I have shared my insights through the years in a series of talks titled, "The Art of Happy Living."™ The talks cover everything from mindfulness to resiliency to stress relief.

In an effort to share these messages with you, I wanted you to know me. Sharing with one another helps break down barriers. I'm hoping you will connect with me. So I have worked with my dear friend, Kelly Dyer Fry, to craft the stories of my life. Kelly is a talented writer and a compassionate person. Together we started with my early years in India and travelled through time. You will find each chapter followed by lessons I have learned.

The world has been my teacher. I want to share the knowledge I have gained over time.

I hope you enjoy reading this book and choose to share it with others.

May God bless you in a vibrant and peaceful journey.

– R. Murali Krishna, M.D.

ACKNOWLEDGMENTS

I am deeply grateful to so many who have been such a part of my journey and my life.

First to Jay Shurley, M.D., who invited me to come to Oklahoma City and to Dr. Agustín Lopez, who was kind and wise in convincing my wife, Sam, that we should make Oklahoma City our home.

To my first partners – Charles Smith, Jr., M.D. and Robert Outlaw, M.D. of Professional Corporation of Psychiatry for taking a chance on a "brown man with an accent" to join their practice. And to my current partners – John Andrus, M.D. and Amal Chakrabutty, M.D. whose support and friendship have sustained me throughout several decades.

To my colleagues at St. Anthony Hospital for having confidence in me to help steer our hospital's response to the devastating Oklahoma City bombing of the Alfred P. Murrah Federal Building.

To Stan Hupfeld who had the vision to build mental health programs at INTEGRIS Mental Health and asked me to help guide and grow that vision. I am deeply grateful for his guidance, friendship and unshackled trust and belief in me. To Bruce Lawrence, James White, M.D. and Chris Hammes, INTEGRIS Health, for their sustained support and friendship for all the ventures we have undertaken.

To Jim Hall, Reverend William Carpenter, William Hawley, M.D., Charlotte Lankard, Patricia Price-Browne and Gene Barth for their shared vision with me to create and sustain the

James L. Hall, Jr. Center for Mind, Body and Spirit. And to the advisory board members for their continued commitment and involvement in the Center.

To our staff at INTEGRIS, without whose help I could not have accomplished our goals and dreams, especially Lynn Horton, Jim Igo and Susie Waugh. Susie has been by my side for every major professional endeavor since 1978. And to Pam Jones, without whose help this book would not have been written.

To my many friends and colleagues in the community of Oklahoma City: Dr. Terry Cline, Oklahoma Commissioner of Health; Terri White, Commissioner of the Oklahoma Department of Mental Health & Substance Abuse Services; Jay Cannon, M.D.; Ira Schlezinger; D. Robert McCaffree, M.D. – Oklahoma County Medical Society and Health Alliance for the Uninsured; Mark Mellow, M.D. – James L. Hall, Jr. Center for Mind, Body & Spirit; Rev. Karrie Oertli, D.Min. – James L. Hall, Jr. Center for Mind, Body & Spirit; Jane Teague, RN – Professional Corporation of Psychiatry; Jana Timberlake, Tomás Owens, M.D. – Oklahoma County Medical Society and other esteemed colleagues with the Oklahoma County Medical Society; Pam Cross with the Health Alliance for the Uninsured and its board members; M. Dewayne Andrews, M.D., Senior Vice President and Provost, and Executive Dean, College of Medicine at The University of Oklahoma Health Sciences Center and Rhonda Sparks, M.D. for their roles in stimulating and nurturing the medical students' interest in volunteerism in the community; Jackie Jones and Sue Hale who were instrumental in the formation of Central Oklahoma Turning Point. Thank you all for encouraging me to strive for the impossible.

To Michelle May, M.D. for giving me insightful feedback about the book and to Sudhir Khanna, M.D. and Susan Dragoo for their friendship and helpful feedback.

To my wonderful family: Sam, Bindu, Atul, Raja, Sreele and grandchildren – Leela, Sanjiv, Ajay, Rohin, Anish, who love me every day, inspire me and keep my sense of wonder alive.

To my good and dear friend Kelly Dyer Fry who pushed me and encouraged me to be open with this book – and for her talent in putting thoughts on paper in such a vivid way.

I hope you enjoy the book.

– R. Murali Krishna, M.D.

TESTIMONIALS

"Dr. Krishna is a living example of the resilience that can grow from adversity and the positive change that one can create despite exceptional hardship. Through his personal story, he radiates a profound joy for life and helping others which is both insightful and inspiring. During a time of my own personal tragedy and self-doubt, Dr. Krishna's book reminded me that through our struggles we can cultivate our spirit and that, slowly but surely, joy can find its way back into our hearts. His book gave me hope and helped me rediscover my own passion and purpose. I have no doubt that the core message of 'Vibrant' will deeply resonate with many, as it certainly did with me."

– Erin Walling, student and aspiring physician

"Dr. Murali Krishna is truly an Oklahoma treasure. He may have been born in India, but we proudly claim him as an Oklahoman. I was moved by his personal story and willingness to share his joys and his sorrows. Anyone reading this book will feel like he's a longtime friend with sage advice. Make the time to read this thought-provoking book. You'll be glad you did!"

– The Honorable Mary Fallin, Governor of Oklahoma

"Dr. Murali Krishna selflessly shares the captured lessons of his life through his own personal journey. His experiences, both joyful and tragic, poignantly reach out to touch us where we are in our lives in a very universal way. In a very gentle and moving approach, he guides us to seek a spirit of living in the present, being grateful for our lives and those lives that we have the potential to touch."

- *Jenny Alexopulos, D.O., Associate Dean of Clinical Services, Professor of Family Medicine, Oklahoma State University – Center for Health Sciences, Tulsa, Oklahoma*

"'Vibrant' reveals the Murali Krishna I know. Although a loyal friend, outstanding clinician, and generous colleague, he is foremost a visionary. Murali is at his best when he is creating and implementing his ideas for a better future. Time and again he has foreseen the direction health care was going and has not just had ideas for the betterment of society but has always brought together and led the people and resources to actually bring about real and lasting good."

- *John Andrus, M.D., President, Professional Corporation of Psychiatry*

"Dr. Krishna's 'Vibrant' gives us that rare opportunity to look into the window of the author's soul and experience how perfectly his life events are attached to his beliefs, his heart and his teachings. This book will have a meaningful impact on the reader's life journey."

- *Arnold C Bacigalupo, Ph.D., President, Voyageur One, Inc.*

"A delightful read in one sitting or immerse yourself theme at a time and let that light take hold in your consciousness. With the same story-telling gift of his Thatha (grandfather), Murali Krishna opens the doors to each of life's major transitions and blessings. As he says, there are no inventions... just discoveries of the magnificence of the Creator, in all realms - physical, spiritual, and mental. 'Vibrant' is a gift of hope and sensibility. Take for yourself and share."

- *Laura Boyd, Ph.D., CEO – Policy and Performance Consultants, Inc.*

"Dr. Krishna allowed me to read his new book several months ago. Following his journey from India to INTEGRIS Health has revealed to me what has made him such a warm, caring, and effective physician. I both laughed and cried while reading the book. His life has shown that pain can be turned into gain. Murali is a vibrant force in the lives of all of those who know him and are privileged to call him a friend."

- Jay P. Cannon, MD, Chief of Staff, INTEGRIS Baptist Medical Center

"From one brown man with an accent to another" - Dr. Krishna's encouragement, mentoring and nurturing of me and my family has been instrumental in realizing our own American dreams. The title of his book, 'VIBRANT – TO HEAL AND BE WHOLE' – From India to Oklahoma City, speaks volumes in itself! Each chapter revealed a very touching, moving, and inspirational story of his life journey full of both joy & pain that molded him into the caring, compassionate and visionary physician of today. If you want to know how to live a VIBRANT life, read this book!"

- Amal Chakraburtty, MD, FAPA, Clinical Professor of Psychiatry; OU
College of Medicine

"Dr. Krishna's life story transported me thousands of miles to another country and culture, across decades of time and tradition, while simultaneously helping me understand what is closest, my own heart and thoughts. A truly touching and inspirational story with transformational power!"

- Terry Cline, Ph.D., Oklahoma Commissioner of Health, Secretary of
Health and Human Services

"From my first awareness of Dr. Krishna's healing methods during a workshop on managing stress, given at a conference on HIV/AIDS, my life has been enriched and nourished by his words, his actions, and his most genuine caring nature. His book provides a powerful look into his life and his heart. Thank

you for sharing so generously so that others may experience
renewal of spirit."

*– Pamela S. Cross, MPH, Executive Director, Health Alliance for the
Uninsured*

"Through Murali Krishna's life story, we get a peek into the
forces that coalesced to create this incredible man. Although
he has faced incredible adversity and hardship during his
lifetime, he radiates joy and optimism. 'Vibrant' is a testament
on how to live a happy, moral and purposeful life."

– Chris Hammes, Executive Vice President and COO, INTEGRIS Health

"Murali Krishna has a wonderful and inspiring way of
educating us on the true meaning of happiness and hope. This
book is a 'must read' for every one of us that has experienced
pain in our lives and want to heal. Murali, thank you for
making an impact on the lives of so many."

– Debby Hampton, President & CEO, United Way of Central Oklahoma

"Murali Krishna is really an Ambassador of Peace. Not
peace between countries but peace between the conflicting
feelings and instincts in the human spirit. His long and
fascinating life journey and the perspective gained as well as
his scholarly expertise have combined to create an insightful
book that is a roadmap to a vibrant life. He has given us all a
lasting gift by sharing his remarkable insights with us all."

– Burns Hargis, President, Oklahoma State University

"These stories told by Murali Krishna are an engaging
journey through sorrow and resiliency to joy and contentment.
There are vivid lessons within for those who make the time
to read the book with thoughtful consideration. As I read
his book I relived the many occasions on which he has been
encourager, supporter, counselor, and mentor and, most often,
friend. To be blessed is to have encountered individuals who

have changed your life for the better. Murali Krishna is one of those blessings in my life."

- Lynn Horton, CFA, System Vice President, INTEGRIS Health

"Since 1996 when Dr. Murali Krishna came to INTEGRIS Health it has been my privilege to work with him, and to come to know him as my friend. Through his book, 'Vibrant,' Murali gives our community, as well as countless others across the nation, the experience of recognizing the healing that can come from the mind-body-spirit connection. He truly has mastered the art of happy living, and skillfully shares his life story to benefit others."

- Stanley F. Hupfeld, FACHE, Chairman, INTEGRIS Foundation

"This book is honest and wise.   It is a wisdom that does not come from books but from a life that has experienced both sorrow and joy, fear and hope, helplessness and resilience.

It is a look behind the cheerful smile and the warm hug of Dr. Krishna into the heart and mind of a small boy, a teenager and a mature adult as he faced difficult life challenges.   Rather than be defeated by them, he has found a way to make his experiences useful to others."

- Charlotte Lankard, Marriage & Family Therapist; weekly columnist for The Oklahoman; and author of "It's Called Life"

"Murali Krishna is one of the most inspiring and genuine people I have ever met. His magnanimous heart and vibrant personality instills in everyone he encounters a sense of caring, compassion and hope for the future."

- Bruce Lawrence, President   & CEO, INTEGRIS Health

"'Vibrant' shares the fascinating life journey and the inspiring life lessons of a compassionate and insightful physician and leader. Murali Krishna's words transported me to a land far away, then back again, all the while weaving in the universal truths that guide each of us toward love, joy, and peace no matter what the external circumstances."

- Michelle May, M.D., author of "Eat What You Love, Love What You Eat"

"It is a great thrill for us to see our dear friend Murali put to print his thoughts about his approach to life. Murali is truly one of those unique individuals who brings a sense of joy and harmony to those in his presence."

- Mark Mellow, M.D., James L. Hall, Jr. Center for Mind, Body & Spirit

"Dr. Murali Krishna is an amazing human being who has discovered how to stand on the threshold between matter and spirit, science and faith, knowledge and wisdom, fact and truth, the mysterious and the miraculous, the commonplace and the wondrous. And he does so with such uncommon grace and kindness that it both touches and delights the hearts of those who come to know him."

- Dr. Norman Neaves, Senior Minister Emeritus, Church of the Servant (UMC), Oklahoma City, OK

"'Vibrant' is the awe-inspiring chronicle of a life of purpose. Murali Krishna melds the quotidian with the sublime in a seamless parable of single-mindedness, tenacity and determination: not toward reaping the spoils of success, but rather towards meeting the salutary joy that is revealed by the glory of giving. For that, Oklahoma has been very blessed to call him an adopted son."

- Tomás P. Owens, M.D., President, Oklahoma County Medical Society. Clinical Professor, OU Health Sciences Center

"Dr. Krishna is well known for his delightful talks, both to physicians and the general public, explaining with solid scientifically-based studies how greater health of the mind and spirit can lead to better physical health.

This book is a compilation of the important information

in those talks interspersed with his story of growing up in India and coming to America as a distinguished physician. He explains how mental illness has saddened his family as it has saddened so many of our families.

He shows how balance, being upbeat, optimism, calmness, having a fulfilling relationship, and finding some joy in each day leads to even more happiness as well as reducing physical illness.

If we could all follow the concepts he writes about in such an interesting way, we could reduce so much mental and physical distress. Five stars and two thumbs up!"

- John A. Robinson, M.D., President, Oklahoma State Medical Association

"Murali does a fabulous job of weaving accounts of his actual life experiences with the incredible wisdom he has been able to derive from them. He presents sage advice that can easily be applied to all of our lives if we're honest with ourselves. This is easily digestible psychotherapy in a book... without the couch, the resistance or the expense. Murali goes down easy in this book, just like he does for each of us that get to work with him in person... every day and in every situation. Remarkable!"

- James P. White, MD, CMO, Managing Director, INTEGRIS Health

"Dr. Krishna's powerful and moving personal stories help all of us think about how we're living our own lives. The thoughts, lessons and reminders that he so caringly conveys provide an opportunity to contemplate our own happiness, purpose and presence. A wonderful gift from a truly wonderful human being."

- Terri White, Commissioner, Oklahoma Department of Mental Health and Substance Abuse Services

"Okay, turn off the TV! Put up the computer, hide your cell phone! I know you think you're too busy to read a book, but you can't afford NOT to read this one! Dr. Murali Krishna knows how busy people are, but he also knows that in today's fast paced society, most of us are too often stressed, sleepless and depressed. What does one do? Is there hope? Read his book, you will see there is reason to hope. How can you find peace and happiness in today's hectic world? Read his book! As one who has lost his first born son, I personally know the pain and depression that follow. Murali's life experiences show he, too, has faced and overcome similar obstacles. You can as well. Peace and wellbeing await within!"

- Reggie N. Whitten, Chairman of Pros for Africa and Whitten Newman Foundation

"Dr. Krishna, inspires us all to look at life through a variety of lenses. He represents all that is good and right in the world. His gift of wisdom and love transcends all boundaries and binds us from the east to the west and beyond. 'Vibrant' is Dr. Murali Krishna!"

- Avilla T. Williams, President, INTEGRIS Health Edmond

"Dr. Krishna's personal story 'Vibrant' is an inspiring and thoughtful journey from rural India years ago to present day Oklahoma City, where he continues his work to improve the lives of all Oklahomans. His life lessons and insights continue to resonate throughout his tireless efforts to make a positive difference in the physical, mental, and spiritual well-being of his patients, colleagues, and every person he encounters. I am honored to know and work with Dr. Krishna, and am reminded of Proverbs 22:29: 'Do you see a man who excels in his work? He will stand before Kings.' Dr. Krishna is such a man."

- Ron Woodson, MD, Cardiologist, Vice President Oklahoma State Board of Health

DISCLAIMER

The contents of this book are based on the experiences, observations, learnings, thoughts and insights of only R. Murali Krishna, M.D. and should not be construed as medical or psychological advice. The contents of this book may or may not apply to you or anyone you know. Anyone who may currently suffer from medical or psychological dysfunction should consult with a trained physician or mental health professional to obtain an evaluation and an appropriate course of treatment. Neither the publisher nor the author take any responsibility or liability for any possible consequences from any action, treatment, or application of principles by any person reading the following information in this book.

VIBRANT
TO HEAL AND BE WHOLE
From India to Oklahoma City

BY R. MURALI KRISHNA, M.D.

WITH KELLY DYER FRY

MCKINLEY BROWNE PUBLISHING

He used to tell me, "Murali, if you have a house,
it can burn down. If you have jewels, they can be stolen.
The only thing that cannot be taken from you
is what you have in your brain."

CHAPTER ONE

A SMALL BOY IN INDIA

Quiet.

No talking now. Wait.

As a young boy, R. Murali Krishna sat stone still on his grandfather's lap as he watched him place one finger over a nostril and slowly inhale. Murali, with head bowed back, watched his grandfather's finger nestle into his large mustache. He watched his chest and abdomen rise. Then fall. He watched his nostrils flare. He could hear the soft whistle of his breath.

Hold.

Wait.

His fingers moved slowly to release one nostril and cover the other. Breathe out. Wait. Time stood still.

Murali affectionately called his grandfather Thatha. They often sat on the verandah of his grandfather's home. He remembers climbing the many steps up to the big rock doors. The verandah was just to the left. Men from the community often gathered there for prayer or conversation. It was there

At left, Murali sits in Gandhi Nagar Park in Kakinada. As a young boy he often went there for some quiet time.

where he often observed his grandfather sitting with his spine straight in quiet reflection, covering one nostril at a time to practice Pranayama. It was just one of many breathing meditations Murali watched with wonder. Pranayama translates in English to "life force … to practice to become perfect," says the now Dr. R. Murali Krishna. "It is not just air. It is life force."

It was on the verandah where Murali learned his first English word.

"Angel," said Thatha with careful pronunciation.

"An-gel," said Murali with slow precision. "What does it mean, Thatha?"

In his native language of Telugu, the grandfather explained that angel was a spiritual figure.

"Now write it here," he said as he handed Murali a slate. A N G E L, Murali wrote the letters very carefully.

Angel.

He had watched his grandfather sit and write for hours. He carried his prayer book wherever he went. It was more than writing. It was Rama Koti, the practice of writing God's name 10 million times. Thatha's books contained the same two words over and over and over. "Sri Ram." With each word, the grandfather pictured a loving act by God. He pictured His face. He pictured Him feeding the poor. He pictured Him caring for the sick. The stack of books grew. He filled book after book. He filled shelves. By the end of his life, he had completed his Rama Koti. Often, the sacred books are placed within the columns of new temples. Sadly, Murali has no copies today. But he holds dear so many memories of his grandfather.

Memories of another era -- another country.

He remembers his grandfather's easy chair. It had wide wooden arms that would swing inward to form a writing surface. He remembers his prayer beads, the mala. He held the 108 beads in his hands as he went through the prayers. The one in 108 represents "One God." The zero symbolizes the "completeness of God" and the eight represents the central traits of God: Power, kindness, luminance, abundance, strength, omnipotence, omnipresence and omniscience.

Murali loved to spend time with his grandfather, especially after his mother became ill. Thatha was a very wise man, but even he had no answers for Murali regarding his mom — or Amma, as she was called.

Getting up early in the morning was never a strong suit for young Murali, but the one thing that could get him up and going was the promise of a walk to the gardens with his grandfather. The 3-mile walk was punctuated by snacks of black, purplish berries plucked along the roadside. But mostly the walks were filled with questions. And Murali had many questions for his Thatha.

"What's that bird, Thatha? Who is God? Where is God? Why are some people untouchable?"

At that time, India was still operating under a caste system. Priest and Warrior families were at the top. They were followed by merchants. Cleaners, cobblers, etc. were among the lowest ranks. And then there were the untouchables.

Thatha's life lessons for young Murali consistently centered on human kindness. Murali learned quickly from his grandfather that he did not adhere to the demarcations of a caste system

"'You've got to be kind to people,' he told us over and over and over."

The aging grandfather did more than share his wisdom; he taught by example.

"He stopped on our walks to talk to all kinds of people.

Cobblers. Cleaners. People who cleaned lavatories."

He reminded Murali, his siblings and young cousins that they came from a good family, a loving family; a family of some privilege.

"He used to tell us to be concerned for people. Ask if they are hurting."

That message stuck with Murali. Even at his young age, he knew his mother was hurting. He just did not know why.

On the walks to the gardens, there were two lakes along the way. They stopped often to watch flocks of white birds take off. They occasionally saw green parrots with red beaks. Some families captured the treasured birds and taught them to talk.

What are they? How did they teach them? Why?

Thatha seemed to have all the answers and never tire of Murali's questions. He also seemed to be ahead of his time.

"He was a great recycler. Can you believe that? He wore shoes made out of tires. He took an old tire to the cobbler and used it for the soles of his sandals. He would make three pairs a year, and that is all he wore. He would also give them to his friends."

As they neared their destination, Murali could smell the mangos. With more than 100 varieties, mangos are India's national fruit. His grandfather and two uncles owned the 16-acre garden. Jasmine dotted the gardens and mixed with the smell of mangos. Part of the garden was planted with mangos and the other part grew sapota, a kiwi-like fruit. Thatha would reach high into the tree and pull a branch down. He would reach into his pocket and fish out his pocketknife. He always carried a pocketknife along with his pocket watch. Murali watched as his grandfather dusted the green mango off on the front of his shirt and then slice it before adding a touch of salt, pepper and chili powder. Sour. Salty. Spicy. Firm. Another variety of mango was taken home to be ripened in straw for a few days. When it became soft, they would squeeze it to make the insides mushy, then cut a hole in the top and suck out the sweet pulp.

For a young boy, the garden held adventure and love. Love for the fruit and love between a young boy and his grandfather.

Education. Education. Education.

Murali got the message repeatedly from his grandfather.

"He used to tell me, 'Murali, if you have a house, it can burn down. If you have jewels, they can be stolen. The only thing that cannot be taken from you is what you have in your brain.'"

That same message was repeated to Murali by his father, though his father took a much different approach. While his grandfather's message was filled with praise, Murali's father often down played his son's success. Murali could hear his father talking among his friends.

"He would say, 'I'll be lucky if he goes to college.' It would make me so mad, and my mother mad too. I would challenge him. I didn't understand."

As Murali grew older, he realized his father's humility was rooted in the fact that he believed it was a bad omen to brag about one's children.

His father also echoed Thatha's message about the importance of God and spirituality.

"My father also had a strong message. 'Live an honorable life with honesty and dignity. Fight for what is right. Never ever give up on God. You have never done anything wrong to other people. God will always reward you, so hang on to Him in the depths of your sorrows.' My father used to say that. I prayed so hard. My prayer was always, 'God, don't let my father fall apart.'"

Murali knew his father was holding the family together.

Happy people like themselves. They feel
they have something to offer and they like to know they are
contributing. Being a productive citizen of the world
gives us a sense of accomplishment.

CHAPTER TWO

DR. R. MURALI KRISHNA
ON HAPPINESS

Today is part of your life's journey.

Don't miss it.

We live our lives at a high rate of speed. We tell ourselves we will be happy if we get the house, get the car, get the wife or get the husband. We will surely be happy when we get our dream job. But wait, how about the corner office? Now look, there's a better car.

If we focus just beyond our reach, there is always something out of our grasp. Don't miss what is right in front of you. Happy people do more than acknowledge what is in front of them, they learn to savor and appreciate it.

They learn to smell the flower, pet the dog and admire the sunrise.

Every life has challenges. If you think the family down the street has a pain-free life, you are mistaken. Life is filled with peaks and valleys. But you can find happiness in either.

Life's journey brings with it certain milestones. I will be happy when I get to start school. I will be happy when I get to middle school. I will be joyous when I can drive a car. I cannot wait until I am 21. But reality tells us that our teen years, though happy and carefree, can be angst-filled and awkward. Our 20s can be exciting, but are also filled with job changes and the stress of finding a spouse. Even retirement years bring their own sets of problems. Do I have enough money? Do I have a support system? For some, retirement is a lonely time – a time of isolation.

Age alone has little impact on happiness.

In the same way, gender plays no role in happiness. Neither sex is happier than the other. Men and women socialize differently, but they also have different levels of need. For example, women may gain more benefit from having a lot of friends. But at the end of the day, no gender has a corner on the market on happiness.

And money? One of the most common themes associated with happiness is money. But money is vitally important to happiness only when it is being spent on the most basic life necessities: food, shelter and health care. Once these basic needs are met, money loses much of its power. Happiness is not necessarily having what you want; happiness is wanting what you have. Tangible purchases bring pleasure for approximately 90 days. But experiences are remembered far longer. It is not what you buy that makes you happy, but what you experience in life. For example, a wonderful trip will give you lasting memories, but the pleasure of a new car will wane in just three months.

The Rolling Stones said it well:

You can't always get what you want

But if you try sometimes, you just might find

You get what you need

Genetics also play a strong role in our happiness. About 50 percent of our happiness quotient is determined by genetics. Ten percent is based on life experiences and 40 percent is derived from our own volition. We can choose to be happy.

When I was in medical school, our days and nights were

filled with studying. I took great joy late into the evenings when I broke away from my studies to sit on a little balcony at the back of our apartment. Below us was a little hut where several musicians lived. They scattered during the day to pick up work and maybe bring home a little food to share. Everything they had was shared with one another. After their evening meal together, they began to sing and play. Every night was filled with joy. They were practicing a play about good kings and bad kings. I don't know if they ever performed it anywhere or not. It didn't matter, for their joy came not from performing, but practicing. They found happiness in their journey.

Each member of the group was concerned for the whole, not just for themselves.

If we are more focused on others than ourselves, we will find it can bring us contentment.

Happy people like themselves. They feel they have something to offer and they like to know they are contributing. Being a productive citizen of the world gives us a sense of accomplishment.

Happy people feel they can make a difference in the lives of others. It is not that they want to control others, but they have a sense that they can contribute in a positive way. They like to feel a part of something larger than themselves and know how they fit in. They recognize the importance of connecting with those around them.

Optimism is a characteristic of happy people. They look for positives in people, places and things. Even in our darkest times, we can often see good coming from a bad situation. Sometimes the lesson may be unclear at the time, but can be seen many years later as life unfolds.

Happy people are close to others. We all need connection.

The most important aspect is to have a close, trusting relationship with others. Isolation does not lend itself well to being happy.

Spirituality is one of the keys to being happy. We need to believe in the intangibles that add meaning and value to our lives. There is something beyond us. The more I learn of science, the more I believe in God. In fact, I have come to the conclusion in my own mind that science is God. He is the ultimate and supreme power. We are only seeing a glimpse of that power. Man congratulates himself on inventions, but we only make discoveries -- not inventions. Electricity was there all the time before it was discovered. The ability to float was there since the beginning of water, but it took perhaps millions of years before man recognized it and built boats. All knowledge is in existence, we continue to uncover facts and put God's elements together in new and different ways.

Happy people tend to have balance in their lives. In our fast-paced world, it is easy to spend too much time working and not enough time relaxing and recharging. Work, play and spirituality are all components we need in our lives to be happy. If any of the three begins to dominate, we can quickly become out of balance. It is important to live life deliberately. Happy people take note of the balance in their lives.

Creativity can play an important role in our happiness. You don't have to be a grand artist or musician, but you need to be creative in thought. Look for problems from a variety of viewpoints. Be a creative problem solver. Creative people do not let life stand still. They continue to seek out new ideas. They pursue new experiences and seek to explore and gain understanding.

It is within us all to be happy. Being happy is a fundamental right of all humans. Not only is it a right, it is essential to our overall health and wellbeing. The relationship between mind, body and spirit is central to our health.

Proverbs 17:22 says that "A merry heart doeth good like a medicine…"

Written thousands of years ago, that ancient proverb is still rock-solid today.

To this day, I say there is a test to see
if someone is a happy person. If they show pleasure
at someone else's success and if they can show concern
when someone is suffering or hurting, then
they are truly a happy person.

CHAPTER THREE

A LITTLE SIBLING RIVALRY, A LITTLE MISCHIEF

It started with a little tickle in his throat.

Then it was moving.

Squirming.

Murali reached into his mouth and pulled out a worm.

His aunt stood there wagging her finger. "I told you so."

The toddler had been sneaking into the kitchen and grabbing handfuls of sugar. It was another example of young Murali acting out. His baby sister had arrived and turned his world upside down. Rama Devi was now getting all the attention. But at least his mother was healthy and happy — for now.

Sibling rivalry. Rebellion.

"I'm not sure what it was. It must have been a roundworm. My aunt was so mad at me. She came to help my mom with the new baby. Her main job was to try and stop me from eating sweets. I would reach up to the counter and grab anything I could. The worm scared me. That's what finally got me to stop."

That memory is one of many for Murali. Other memories center on his new baby sister.

At left, Murali poses with his mom, dad and two sisters in Rampachodavaram.

"I remember thinking, 'That little thing comes along and gets all the attention.'"

Then there was the memory of the lost fruit tree.

"There were two fruit trees in our yard. We called them jama trees. It's a green fruit — really sweet. It is similar to the guava fruit that is sold now in the Asian stores and Mexican stores. One tree had really sweet fruit we used to eat. The second tree was not as sweet. My father removed the sweet tree because it was too close to the roof. I didn't understand why he took it away."

First the baby, then the tree. Three-year-old Murali's world was turned upside down.

And that was just the start of it.

His parents made great sacrifices and scraped together enough money to send their only son to a private pre-school. It was a convent. The uniform for the school was a crisply-starched white cotton shirt and dark navy blue shorts. His parents were excited about the big day. Murali was not.

A rickshaw pulled up in front of their house to take the little boy to school. Murali would have no part of it.

His mother grabbed his hand to escort him to the waiting "driver." Pulling away from his mom's grip, Murali dropped to the ground and rolled in the red dirt. He was covered head to toe in sticky dirt. Back inside he went. Another bath. Another set of clean clothes. This time he was *carried* directly to the rickshaw.

Murali arrived at the school and found that everyone had matching clothes. There was a nun dressed in a full black habit. She glided across the floor as her habit swished. It looked like she had no feet. She had a kind face, but there was no smile. Serious. Perfectly still.

"I remember there was no talking, no laughter. I felt I did

not fit in."

Every morning, it was the same routine. The starched white shirt. The clean shorts. Red dirt. Another bath. After only a few days of wrestling with the youngster, his parents surrendered. Murali was moved to a government school.

"I loved it. I fit right in."

The government school was loud and chaotic. The teacher carried a rod and didn't hesitate to line *everyone* up for a whack if he could not nail down the single instigator.

"Looking back on it, I wonder if in the back of my mind I knew the convent was such a financial hardship for my parents."

His father was working as a clerk at the time. He was making very little money, and they could not find a cheaper house to rent.

"In India there was no rental standard. It depended on how much money the owner needed rather than what the house was worth."

His maternal grandfather grew concerned for his daughter and her young family. He came to visit us and walked the streets for days to find more suitable housing. Murali's father was spending half his earnings on rent, leaving little money to feed and care for his family.

"For days and days and days, my grandfather walked the streets until he found a new home for us. Everything in India is about family. That was monumental. It left a lasting impression on me."

One of the highlights of the grandfather's trip was Akshara Abhyasam. The special Indian ceremony introduces young children to the world of learning. Akshara translates to "letters." Abhyasam means "practicing to become perfect."

It was a special day. Murali was dressed in nice clothes

while waiting for the special moment between grandfather and grandson.

Dry rice was mixed with turmeric.

Blessings.

Prayers.

It was spread on a large round plate. Grandfather took Murali's small hand in his. With his index finger, he traced through the yellow rice while saying "Om" in a slow low voice. According to custom, "Om" is the first sound uttered in the universe. They slowly wrote the figures in Telegu.

O M.

They prayed to Saraswathi, the goddess of learning.

The story of his grandfather coming to find their new house was repeated to young Murali throughout his childhood.

"It made an impression on me. It demonstrated such an act of caring. To this day, I say there is a test to see if someone is a happy person. If they show pleasure at someone else's success and if they can show concern when someone is suffering or hurting, then they are truly a happy person. My grandfather showed such great concern for us. It was a valuable lesson."

School started to go well for young Murali. He soared through kindergarten and first grade. He remembers the black slate with the pencil they called a balapam.

"We wrote our letters over and over and over on the slates."

But it was when they started writing numbers and doing multiplication tables that he started to shine.

"I found that math came very easy to me. I was fast."

Teachers soon caught on to his advanced skills. One day his parents came to the school. With much excitement and fanfare, they were told their second grader should be promoted early to the third grade.

"They were joyful."

But the walk from one class to another was filled with anxiety for Murali.

"I was leaving my friends behind. Now everyone was older and much bigger. It was like a mechanical event for me. I felt scared.

"I learned some adaptive skills — mostly how to run fast so I could get away from the bigger boys. My athletic skills never involved size or muscles, but quickness."

Murali spent only 6 months in the third grade before the early promotion struck again. He was once again moved up to the next grade and was now getting a lot of attention for his school work. This made his Thatha very proud.

"I found what made my grandfather proud, and it motivated me."

When Murali was not showing off his multiplication skills – "12 times 12 is 144" – he was showing off his newfound running skills. The big boys still picked on him, but he could *still* outrun them. And, surely if he could run fast, he could eventually fly.

"I used to think as a child that somehow you could fly."

That childlike belief led him to many flying experiments.

Murali took palm leaves and spread them wide before attaching them to his chest. His friends watched as he leapt from a ledge.

"If you run fast with the wind at your back, it feels like you fly a little bit."

Even now, the distinguished doctor gets a far-off look when he thinks about his flying attempts. A slow smile spreads across his face.

Another favorite pastime was making and flying kites. Newspapers were tied to bamboo sticks. The boys ran through the village with homemade kites soaring behind them.

"The whole place was like a park. Anywhere there was

space, we played."

If they weren't flying kites, they were rolling tires.

"We would roll them down the middle of the streets. We raced along beside them."

There weren't many cars, so the streets were fair game for running or playing cricket.

"We set up to play cricket anywhere we wanted. If a car came, which wasn't very often, we just moved everything aside."

His father's cousin had one of the few cars he knew of. The small black car resembled an English taxi, only much smaller.

"I remember it had a crank on the front to start it."

Murali piled into the car with his father and his cousin who had two young boys. There are still scattered memories of a pond, some goldfish, a water fountain and roses. Special times. Special places.

With no televisions, the children played outside until well into the evening. There was a loud speaker in the park where townsfolk would gather at 7 o'clock to hear the evening news. Radio was a novelty.

Sunday mornings, families would gather around the radio to hear a special children's program.

"It was called Radio Thatha or Radio Grandfather."

Skits and songs crackled to the delight of children.

Storytelling was an important part of Murali's young life in India. When he traveled to his paternal grandfather's house, he sought out one of Thatha's administrative helpers.

"We had to bribe him with fruit or pocket coins so he would tell us scary stories."

Many of the stories focused on good and evil.

"The mythology gave me strong roots in knowing good and bad, true and false or truth and lies. The importance of really doing good to people."

The myths were 5,000 to 6,000 years old. It was oral tradition.

"I have always been fascinated by the themes."

Though the world changes, the basic principles of good and evil have remained throughout the centuries.

Thatha's house always held surprises for Murali — like the time his grandfather took cardboard to make a sort of can that was tied to string. Murali was on one end and Thatha was on the other. String stretched through the house.

"I was astounded when I could hear his voice."

His grandfather took note of his grandson's delight. He knew how much Murali loved spending summers with him.

"He would say, 'Don't get too settled down, Murali. You have a guaranteed return ticket on your train. You will go home when school starts.'

I later realized he was not only talking about my return trip after summer vacation, he was talking about my return ticket to heaven. I remind people of that still to this day. We all have a return ticket home. Life is a very short journey."

The answer is not complex. It is simple.
Stay in the present. Be mindful. Be present. Be focused
on what is in front of you.

CHAPTER FOUR

DR. R. MURALI KRISHNA
ON ENJOYING
THE MOMENT

It seems the older we get, the faster life goes.

Mahatma Gandhi said it like this, "There is more to life than increasing its speed."

I remember as a child that summertime seemed to last forever. While childhood can be filled with play, often adulthood can be filled with stress and anxiety. But we can still tap those childlike feelings of exploration. We can continue to discover life, to learn, to grow.

We can learn throughout our lives to savor the moment. We can get more out of right now.

Many of us may be over-focused on what has happened in the past or what may happen in the future. We may not even be aware we are doing it. When we look back or look forward, we can often miss what is happening right in front of us. We literally kill the present.

Ironically, the present is the only thing we can control. Each moment is all we really have.

It is important to learn from the past, but it is also important to not let it distract and take energy from the present.

We often are guilty of looking too far into the future. We react based on things we think might happen. This creates anxiety and tension within us and can negatively impact our present decisions. In short, if you worry too much about the future, your anxiety can impact the decisions you make today.

The answer is not complex. It is simple. Stay in the present.

Be mindful.

Be present.

Be focused on what is in front of you.

We live in a society of screens. Computer screens, television screens, smart phone screens, tablet screens and others. We are "plugged in" 24 hours a day.

We are distracted.

Look around you at a restaurant and notice all the people with their heads down interacting with their phone or laptop. There may be a loved one sitting across the table – a loved one who deserves our focus and attention. Are you present? Are you mindful of the distractions you are allowing to dominate the moment? It's not just in restaurants. How about around the dinner table in your own home? Is the television on? Are you savoring the food?

We have to take inventory and evaluate how we are spending time with our family, friends and loved ones. Take time to enjoy the moment. Enjoy the meal. Interact face-to-face with those you care about.

We can all turn off our devices long enough to get centered, refocused.

I sometimes hear people say they are "too busy" to slow down. But it doesn't take very long to regroup our emotions. And it doesn't take a quiet room with scented candles. You can refocus yourself at any time.

One way to slow down a hectic moment is to focus on your

breathing. Focus on drawing in the cool air through your nostrils. Feel it filling your lungs. Breathe deep and let your belly rise. As you exhale, feel the air that has been warmed by your lungs. You can count each breath to keep your focus on it. Or, you can think a simple word like "relax" or "peace" on each out breath.

Another exercise is to take a long breath through your nostrils. Hold it for a few seconds then pucker your lips and exhale as slowly as you can.

If we take a few moments each day to do these simple breathing exercises, we can train ourselves to relax, focus and enjoy the moment.

"Walking awareness" is another way of re-centering ourselves. It can be outside or even in a long hallway of a busy office building. Notice each step you take. Focus on your step, your stride. Focus on the way you hold your shoulders and bend your knees. Be mindful of your every movement. Relax. Breathe.

These are simple ways of bringing yourself back into the moment.

It can be almost magical when we truly focus on the moment.

If you are moving too fast, stop and ask yourself what is motivating you?

If you are spending all your time in a car driving your children to soccer, baseball, piano and dance lessons, ask yourself why? Are you over-scheduling your child? What is your motivation for all these activities? Find out what your goal is and then determine the proper steps to get there.

Take responsibility for your decisions. Each of us is given 24 hours in a day. How do you want to spend your time? Where is the balance in your day? Did you work? Play? Relax? Enjoy time with those you care about and love? Every second of every day counts. Focus on those seconds.

What are your priorities?

Our to-do lists are often too long. Be realistic. Live your life deliberately. Reduce the number of to-dos to a more realistic level so you can focus on the larger goals in life, like building lasting relationships. Experiences count more than acquiring things or accomplishing a list of errands and tasks.

We have all had moments in life when we experience oneness. A sense of joy envelops us and we notice and savor it. Maybe it was when your child was born. Maybe it was admiring a waving field of golden wheat or a beautiful Oklahoma sunset. It is important to notice those moments of oneness, to savor them. When every cell in your body resonates that "this is good," it recharges us. It also has positive restorative power. It lowers our blood pressure and boosts our immune system. We can train ourselves to notice even the smallest of God's miracles. It is in noticing and savoring these moments that we gain benefit.

So, slow down. Stop moving so fast.

If you were born in 1900, your lifespan may have been only 40 years. Today we live on average into our 80s. Though we have twice the amount of life to live, we fill our lives with too many demands.

Those who came before us lived life at a slower pace. They worked very hard, and many of their tasks were quite time consuming. If we filled our days walking behind a horse to plow our fields, we would be overwhelmed. Technology has improved our lives. You would think with all the advancements, we would have more time to devote to our friends and family.

That is often not the case.

How do you spend your time?

Do you savor the moment?

Ask yourself these questions, and make deliberate decisions.

You cannot control all situations, but you can always control how you respond. You are in control of your own peace of mind.

I learned a valuable lesson from her.
Believe in people before you believe in something different.
Believe in the good in people. Look for the good side.

CHAPTER FIVE

A MOTHER'S LOVE

It's 6 a.m.

Sunrise.

Close to the equator, the sun rises at 6 a.m. It sets at 6 p.m.

Murali's mom, R. Ranga Rajya Lakshmi, is in the kitchen preparing her family's breakfast. Amma, as he calls her, soaked the mixture of white rice and flour overnight so her family could enjoy their morning staple of idli and chutney. Idli is part of a traditional Indian breakfast. Similar in shape to a donut, idli is not sweet, yet very filling.

Amma slips quietly in to gently awaken Murali. She coaxes the young boy to the kitchen for breakfast. The small house has only one bedroom where the whole family sleeps — father, R. Swamy, Amma, Murali and his two sisters

The family can hear the cow man coming down the street – cow in tow. Amma and her children go to oversee the milking of the cow.

"Sometimes, the cow man and his wife tried to slip in a little water if someone was not looking. It would make my mom so mad. She had a little meter to test the milk. They never tried to trick her after that. She was very protective of us. Nutrition was very important."

One component of Murali's nutrition involved a raw egg

At left is R. Ranga Rajya Lakshmi, or Amma, as Murali called her. She was a devoted wife and mother. Her family was the center of her world.

each day. The egg was added to his diet at the insistence of his Thatha after an unsettling incident with a tutor.

Murali was about 4 years old when a tutor came to the house to work with his older sister. His sister already was excelling at school and had a photographic memory, but the family so valued education they wanted to ensure she perform at the highest level.

The subject level was not age appropriate for Murali, but he wanted to join in nevertheless. The tutor challenged him with questions beyond his years and announced to the family that, heaven forbid, the boy is not very bright.

A letter was dashed off to Thatha, and he arrived with a large bottle of pills to boost Murali's intellect.

"To this day, I have no idea what it was. I'm sure it was a mixture of herbs and vitamins. He also insisted I eat a raw egg every day."

Amma would coax the youngster to take the egg. For a time, she kept a hen at the house to ensure the freshness of Murali's egg.

"She held my nose in the beginning, and then I started doing it myself. She would wash the fresh egg, crack it open and pour it in my mouth."

The young mother was devoted to her children. She always put her needs last. In a time when most women in their community had dozens of saris, Amma only kept three or four.

"They were always neat and clean, but she had very few compared to the other mothers."

Amma preferred to buy saris for her daughters' future. At that time, it was common to collect many saris to be worn by the daughters once they married. Men would stack saris high on top of a bicycle and sell them in the streets.

"He would ride down the street and women would call out to

him to come inside their house."

Upon seeing the sari man, Murali would run to him and tell him to keep going.

"That is only small children calling your name. They are trying to trick you. You should not stop here."

It made the sensitive young boy sad to see his mom look through the colorful saris and never buy one for herself.

"She used to laugh about that. 'My boy won't let me buy ANY saris because I won't buy one for myself.'"

Amma's saris sometimes became a hiding place for the shy boy. The cloth flowing over the shoulder, the pamita, served as a little tent to block out the world.

"When we would go places, I would be shy at first and hide there. Also when it was time to go, I would start tugging on it."

The young mother showed great patience — though Murali often put her to the test. There was a young woman that helped out around the house from time to time. One of her jobs was to take a large vessel to the public watering spigot and get drinking water for the family. If Murali was angry, he put sand in the fresh drinking water.

Amma would quietly ask the young woman to go get more water. "He must be upset about something, let me go and find out."

Occasionally, Amma threatened to tell his father when he got home. But that rarely happened.

"She was really, really patient with me."

Amma was not only patient with her son, but with others. When a family heirloom necklace for her daughter's future wedding – which was 15 to 20 years away – went missing, she began investigating. She went to visit the forest dwellers to take advantage of their spiritual powers.

"The forest dwellers had little contact with the modern

world. They held on to their ancient spiritual belief system. The legend was that this person could make the person who stole from you show up on your thumb. Much to my mom's surprise, it was said to be her assistant. She just could not believe that.

"I learned a valuable lesson from her. Believe in people before you believe in something different. Believe in the good in people. Look for the good side."

Amma never found the heirloom, and never accused her assistant.

"She just let it go."

Amma was a compassionate person.

"Kind and caring. That is how I would describe her."

Caring for her family gave her great pleasure. No one could see what was lurking. Daily life was normal.

Evening was the best part of life in India. Children were always playing outside. Mothers prepared dinner early so they could join their friends outside and watch their children play.

About 6:30 or 7, the families went back inside to wash up and get ready for the family meal. Dinner was served at about 8.

In the early years, the family had no table in the kitchen. Banana leaves that had been purchased at the vegetable market were moistened with water and spread out on the floor. Little stools, usually stacked to one side of the kitchen, were placed in a circle. The evening meal was always finished with a small cup of yogurt. The healthy treat was mixed with rice and maybe a little pickle on the side.

"100 percent of Indian families eat this yogurt. I still eat it every day."

Dinner time was filled with laughter and storytelling. Murali and his sisters formed alliances.

"If you don't tell what I did, I won't tell what you did."

Adults would follow their meals with a mouth freshener known as "pan." The small betel leaves were spiced and mildly sweetened. The children would watch as their parents' mouths and lips turned bright red from the after-dinner treat. Murali and his sisters would get a little taste.

"My mouth is redder than yours."

It is rare for children to get a taste of the betel leaves.

"It will dull your intelligence. That is the legend."

Legends are passed down through family members in India. Murali learned most of the stories through his paternal grandfather, Thatha. But he has good memories of his mother's family as well.

The family would load up in a bullock cart to go visit his mom's parents.

A curtain surrounded the cart to shield the women's faces. Women from respected families were not permitted to show their faces when traveling on the road. Deep ruts made it hard for the cart to navigate. Murali knew not to sit too far back or he would be the first to fall out when they hit a big bump.

"It got stuck sometimes and we all got out and had to push."

While visiting once, he was playing with his uncle on one of the empty bullock carts. The uncle would pull down the front polls and hoist Murali in the air. When the poll slipped from his grasp, Murali crashed down and bit through his tongue. Amma scolded the uncle.

"She told him to take me away and not to bring me back until I was comfortable. So he fed me all kinds of sweets and settled me down. When we walked back in the house, my mom bopped him on the head and laughed. She was very playful."

Happy times turned sad at the grandparents' house when Amma's father grew ill. Murali was at his mother's side when her father died.

Everyone is crying. Murali tucks his head beneath his mom's pamita. Such sadness. So many tears. Amma is crying, and it is breaking her son's heart.

The body is carried immediately away to be cremated near the lake. His family offers his body back to God. Rituals are performed. It is beautiful. And sad.

The sadness of Amma scares Murali.

Those fears will eventually return 10 fold.

See everyone as your fellow traveler in life.
Look beyond what we see with our own eyes. Try to view people
from a grander perspective.

CHAPTER SIX

DR. R. MURALI KRISHNA
ON CONNECTION, GRATITUDE AND CLAIMING YOUR SPIRIT

Life has a beginning and an end.

Experiences in our first few months of life can have an impact on our lives to the very end.

But it is our choices in the middle that make us who we are.

How will you react to life's situations? What paths will you take? Do you know how to express yourself, manage your anger and express your gratitude?

I was blessed with kind and loving parents. I formed a strong bond with them at an early age. We all must bond with someone or something – the earlier the better. It might not be a parent; it might be a caregiver. We all have an overwhelming need to connect. Sometimes, it might even be with a pet. Connecting is part of being human.

If you show someone a photo of someone hurting, you can see the mirror neurons light up in the brain. This is an innate response, beyond our conscious awareness. What we feel is their pain. We can also feel someone's pleasure. Think of someone you know who can truly respond to the emotions of others. They can be happy for someone else's good fortune or success. Conversely, they are saddened if they know someone is hurting. These responses are mirror neurons in action and they represent true empathy.

Experience shows us that empathy can be developed with conscious effort. In short, walk in someone else's shoes.

In every life there are highs and lows. Sometimes we get depressed and we can no longer be happy or even sad for others. But if you focus on the areas of life where you are grateful, it can boost your spirits and even your immune system.

Having an attitude of gratitude is important to us. For example, when I sit on my back porch and watch the Oklahoma sunset, I am grateful to live in a clean city where I can see it so clearly. I have been in areas of the world where it is masked by a haze.

One evening, my wife, Sam, and I were admiring the different varieties of pink begonias in our yard. She told me how some of them grow best in the sun and others thrive better in the shade. But a hail storm came later that night and wiped them all out. I took time afterward to be thankful that we had taken a moment the night before to admire their beauty. A gratitude list starts to take shape when you closely watch throughout the day for things to add. It can truly be transforming.

Gratitude fosters hope, compassion and love. It also makes us more open to forgiveness. If we do not forgive those who have harmed us, we will remain their victim. In simple terms, if I don't forgive you, I am doing harm to myself. But once forgiveness is given, the relationship can return to a state of trust.

Forgiveness and gratitude can also lead us to a spiritual pathway. It has profound healing energy that can bring us serenity and peace. We can learn to see the divine presence of the Creator in our fellow human beings. Look for the good in people. See everyone as your fellow traveler in life. Look beyond what we see with our own eyes. Try to view people from a grander perspective.

If you want to serve God, serve other people. As Mother Teresa says, "We can do no great things, only small things with great love."

There are many angles from which to view others. It is like light. There is only one sun, but it casts its light to form many perspectives. If you are facing a dire situation, look for another angle. Understand that over time, you may uncover the deeper meaning. Just take one step toward hope. The absence of hope is a downward spiral. It is not hope versus reality; it is hope with reality. Keep your feet rooted in reality, but allow hope to creep in.

Remember that we can only control our effort. We cannot control the end result.

We have to be mindful of what we can control and let go of the rest.

One thing we can control is our reaction. If we anger easily, we need to analyze our feelings and learn to calm ourselves. There is a plethora of research showing the negative impact that anger has on our hearts. The risk of a heart attack or stroke increases approximately 100 percent in the two hours following an incident of anger. Anger weakens our immune system and can also delay healing.

The first step in dealing with anger is to recognize it. Know the early warning signs. Do you tense up? Does your heart rate quicken? Do you experience a flushed feeling?

Second, determine the source of your anger. We get angry when we feel a sense of powerlessness or injustice. Are you angered by what happened to you or your response to it? Look for any mistaken attitudes or convictions that may be leading to your anger.

Third, hit the pause button. Count. Go for a walk. Remove yourself from the situation. Listen to music. Do anything to calm your mind. Then, examine your expectations. What triggered the anger? Calming yourself does not mean suppressing your anger. That is not dealing with it. If you hang on to your anger, it will eventually break free.

Fourth, look for solutions. Once you've identified what's causing the anger, you must decide to modify the situation or modify your feelings. If you cannot change the situation or adapt to it, you may have to remove yourself from it.

Fifth, find a way to channel your anger in a positive way. Anger can often motivate us to make a positive change. But if your anger comes from a sense of powerlessness, you need to explore the possibility that you may have self-doubt or self-contempt at a deeper level. You can address this with positive self-talk. Ultimately, it is always up to you to decide how you react.

Anger is a normal human emotion. But don't let your automatic response of anger take over. Live your life with deliberate choices and reactions.

She has a strong grip on Murali's right hand.
He's not sure if she is trying to steady herself or comfort him.
His tiny hand may be her only grip on reality.

CHAPTER SEVEN

WHERE IS MY AMMA?

The wooden gate in front of the family home in Kakinada creaks when it opens. That's how Amma knows her children are home from school.

She greets them at the door with a warm smile, homemade crackers and sweetened lemon water. Neighborhood children know the house well. It is a warm house with a red-tiled roof.

Young Murali loved his mom's greeting every day after school. Neighborhood children trailed behind him so they too could share in the after-school treats. The children crowded around the table as she helped them all with their homework. Amma held court. She only had a fifth-grade education, but Murali knew his mother was smart. After homework and a snack, the children returned to the streets to play cricket and soccer while Amma continued preparing the evening meal for her family.

One day, 9-year-old Murali bounds through the creaky gate and through the front door of his two-room house.

Where is my Amma?

Surprised and a little disappointed that his hug and snack are not waiting in the threshold of his home, he goes to the family's

At left, Murali, far right, poses with his family and friends for a quick photo. Children spend long hours playing outside in India. Evenings are filled with laughter and a little mischief.

bedroom. He is stunned by what he sees. His always-vibrant mother, his beautiful loving mother, is lying on the bed staring at the ceiling. She is silent. She won't talk. Something is wrong. Murali had never seen his mother sick.

He's scared. He pokes and prods and gets Amma to respond a little, but she's not the same. He didn't know it then, but life will never be the same. Life is changing. It is changing for everyone. Forever.

After that day, his mother comes and goes without ever leaving the house. The houses in the neighborhood were close together. The shared wall does little to prevent the sounds of Amma from reaching the neighbors. They can hear the young mother rambling incoherently — sometimes loudly. Murali goes from fear to shame and back to fear. His mother is often uncommunicative and unreachable.

Where is my Amma?

One day, young Murali enters the house carrying his school books. No sign of Amma. He lets his books fall to the floor as he goes to the bedroom in search of her. No one. Just empty beds. He can feel his heart quicken, knowing he has only one place left to search. Maybe she is in the backyard in the small bathroom. As he enters the backyard trimmed with rose bushes, he sees his mom.

She is standing in the middle of the yard. Smoke is rising from her yellow sari with black trim. Flames.

She is setting herself on fire.

Murali grabs his mother and hugs her to his chest to smother the flames.

"Amma! Amma!"

He is sobbing. Murali's cries trigger her maternal instinct, overpowering her despair. She quickly begins to tend to her little boy.

Why? Why? How can this be happening to my beautiful mother?

She takes him by the hand and leads him into the house. She is calm, lucid. She removes his white cotton shirt, which is now blackened and singed. She gives him sweetened lemon water and small homemade crackers. When Murali's father returns home from work, he tells his father of the fire. The exchange of pain between father and son is palpable.

That night, the family settles into bed in their small bedroom. Murali's bed is next to his parents. He sleeps very little, rising periodically to check on his mother. In the early dawn, he sees her slip quietly from her bed. His father is still asleep.

Where is my Amma going?

He too slips from the bedroom and begins to follow her outside. He keeps his distance in the beginning. The morning is chilly and no one is on the street. He can see the cow man a couple streets over. Amma keeps walking. She passes the large statue of Gandhi and heads toward the river. The river that is usually bustling with handmade boats hauling bright colored vegetables from one town to another is silent. Colorful boats stacked with potatoes, tomatoes, eggplant and greens have not yet begun their daily rituals. He starts yelling for her to stop.

"Amma! Amma!"

He waves his arms and sees that she is entering the water. She is dressed in a dark sari, and the water is rising around her. The sides of the river are shallow, but the center is rushing. If she reaches the center, she will be swept quickly away.

He won't be able to save her.

Murali rushes into the water behind her as she continues forward. He cannot swim. As the water rises he begins to choke, gasping for breath. He is reaching for his mom, but she is just beyond his grasp.

He lurches forward and manages to wrap his arms around her waist.

He will not let go.

Once again, a mother's love overcomes the depth of her sorrows. She is just two steps away from the swift moving current when her maternal instincts take over.

She stops. She turns. Her son clings to her, choking. She hangs on to her little boy, and they return slowly to shore. Her sari is wet and heavy. They walk hand in hand back toward the Gandhi statue. She has a strong grip on Murali's right hand. He's not sure if she is trying to steady herself or comfort him. His tiny hand may be her only grip on reality. They pause at the statue of Gandhi. Silence. Murali understands at this young age that Gandhi was in search of truth.

What is the truth for my Amma?

The family dynamic has been forever altered. Questions remain unasked.

Unanswered.

What has happened? How will we go on?

Of course they do go on. But the new normal has less laughter. Happy times are stitched together between bouts of sadness.

Deep sadness.

Where is my Amma?

Find someone you trust and open up to them.
It may be a friend, a spouse, a neighbor – find at least one other
human being and share your story with them.

CHAPTER EIGHT

DR. R. MURALI KRISHNA
ON TRAUMA, GRIEF AND LOSS

There are events in life that are seared into our memory. Events that touch our soul.

Trauma.

Death.

Loss.

Events of soul-tearing magnitude can happen at any age, but the ones that happen to us in childhood can have lasting ramifications well into adulthood. Children do not have the mature logic to deal with bad situations. Therefore, the feelings may be left to fester like a boil. Eventually, they must be dealt with.

We must face the pain head on. Examine every aspect of life at the time of the traumatic event. How old were you? Who was in your family? Where did you live? Who were your neighbors? Your friends? Your relatives? What was your support system? Who was caring for you? Was there an adult in your life that you trusted? Who was guiding you, teaching you?

Then try to remember as much as you can about the

traumatic event. Try to picture as much detail as possible. For my own trauma, I had to remember even minor details, like smelling the smoke of my mother's sari on fire. Recall as much as possible.

Finally, share. Find someone you trust and open up to them. It may be a friend, a spouse, a neighbor – find at least one other human being and share your story with them. Share your memories, your pain, your anger and your fears. You may want to join a support group or keep track of your thoughts in a journal. You can always turn to a professional to help you through your journey of discovery and recovery.

As an adult, we have mature logic to re-examine our childhood traumas. I traveled back to India one time and went to the school where I attended as a child. I was amazed at how small it was. Years ago, I was looking at the building through a child's eyes, but as an adult it appeared totally different. The same can be said of childhood trauma, it must be re-examined through adult eyes. Children are so helpless and so trusting. As adults, we can see how innocent they are and ill-equipped to handle life's tragedies and assaults.

Once you have fully examined the trauma, ask yourself how you overcame the tragedy? What strength did you tap into? How did you survive? There must be some reason you made it through. Deep in every human being is core strength. Look for it. Tap into it. Use that same perseverance as an adult to survive and keep going forward.

Self-examination and introspection are central to healing your spirit. A hurt will stay with you at some level, but it is not good to let it impact your daily life. If you are preoccupied with something from your past every second of every minute of every hour of every day, it will have a dampening effect on your functioning, concentration and ability to live a productive life.

Once you understand the roots of where your hurting is coming from, you begin to resolve the internal feelings that are of a dysfunctional nature. Grief is normal, but prolonged grief has a negative impact on us. You can't allow it to be your uppermost thought. And you cannot numb the pain with alcohol or drugs, which will only lead to even larger problems.

If the trauma involves something you feel guilty over, ask forgiveness from the person you harmed. If that is not possible, ask forgiveness from God and move on with your life. We must be brutally honest with ourselves. We learn and grow through suffering.

If you continue to have dominating negative thoughts, try reframing the situation. Look at it from a different perspective. Try to process it differently. You must retrain yourself to push negative thoughts away. This can be done with cognitive restructuring, better known as self-talk. You can repeatedly tell yourself that you have already addressed it and it is time to move on. Training the mind is like training a muscle; it takes repetition. Today is all you can control. Remind yourself that you have acknowledged the past and chosen to move forward with your life. Tap into the core strength that has kept you going all these years.

Pain and struggles can be powerful motivators. Through my mother's suffering, I found my life's work. I look into the eyes of the very sick and I see her looking back at me. Suffering can lead you to a greater purpose. Look for it. Through loss, we gain. If we are victims, we must let go of our resentments in order to reject our victimization.

Often, those who have dealt with trauma choose to take up a cause and try to make a difference in the world. If your trauma deals with the death of a loved one, you can incorporate their spirit within you to honor their life.

I think there is often a misunderstanding in our society that real love means never letting go of the person you lost – never moving on with your life. You must let go and move on. But, you can reframe your life, incorporating their spirit within your life and finding your own individuality. Find what gives you energy and drive toward a goal. By touching one life, you never know how many other lives can also be impacted. It is like a ripple effect.

Anchor your survival in something greater than yourself. Who is breathing for you at night when you are sleeping? Who is healing you? For every cell in your body there are 10 different bacteria, some good, some bad; yet we still survive. Who is taking care of you? Is all this because you are intelligent? No. It is because our Creator is greater than we are.

Throughout my practice, I have prayed each and every night for my patients who were hurting the most. I have asked God to use me as a conduit to reach and heal them. Without fail, the answers come to me. Prayer has helped me help others.

I often remind myself of Mother Teresa's message. God truly comes to us through suffering people.

There is something beyond what
you experience in life. There is something beyond
what you are seeing with your eyes. There will be days
that you will not have this agony. But you have to have hope,
belief in God – belief in the power of the Creator.

CHAPTER NINE

COMING OF AGE

Murali sat on the porch of their home with his sisters, Swarajya Lakshmi and Rama Devi. They were confused. A sense of emptiness enveloped the children. Their pain was raw, palpable. Their security shattered.

Why do bad things happen to good people?

"There is nothing that I see in sight."

Murali was a deep thinker. He shared with his sisters but wondered to himself: *How did this happen? Why? Where are the rewards for being good and kind to others?*

"It's scary to think about the emptiness I felt inside."

Murali compounded his worry with a fear that something might happen to his father. There were days when he felt as if he had already lost his mother.

"In India, single parenting is like you are an orphan. Your opportunities are limited. I felt we were so close to being nobodies. I shared my fears with Thatha, and he assured me we would always have a home with him if we needed one."

Thatha shared something else too.

"He said to me, 'There is something beyond what you experience in life. There is something beyond what you are seeing with your eyes. There will be days that you will not have

At left, Murali in Thatha's village. He wanted to tell his grandfather in person that he had been accepted to medical school.

this agony. But you have to have hope, belief in God – belief in the power of the Creator.'"

Thatha believed strongly in life's ever-changing path. He had a personal experience that rooted him deeply in his faith. It was on one of their long walks that Thatha shared his story with his only grandson.

"He told me about his near-death experience; that's what we would call it today. He told me he died and came back to life. He described how his spirit left his body and he stood before God. A doctor even pronounced him dead. Thatha saw bright lights like a billion suns. His spirit rose to heaven. He said, 'God showed me on big gold tablets all the good deeds I had done. Then he showed me a list of all the things I may not be proud of. *Your mission on earth is not yet finished. You need to go back and do something of your heart with no selfish gain.*'"

Thatha had spent his career collecting taxes for the kingdom. He was very strict, yet fair. After his near-death experience, he transformed his life and retired from his job. He began to study Ayurveda medicine. The ancient form of Indian medicine involved the use of herbs, roots and other natural remedies.

"After a morning walk, people would gather on the verandah of his home. He gave away his medicine for free and often counseled villagers on emotional issues, relationship problems or money woes. I saw tremendous healing there. It is what first influenced me to become a doctor."

However, Murali did not have clarity on his professional direction until almost 10th grade.

"My grades dipped a bit in seventh and eighth grade. I loved sports and played a lot with models. I was fascinated by what I could build with my hands. I loved trucks and space stations."

Thatha noticed the drop in grades and took his grandson for

a long walk and a long talk.

"I remember him saying to me, 'Within the next 36 months your future will be determined. What do you want to be? An engineer? A doctor? A clerk? You have a higher purpose in life and you need to find out what it is.'"

Murali was drawn to be a healer. Maybe he could find an answer for his Amma — his sweet Amma who was still having some good days and some bad days. Living in a house with uncertainty can create layers of anxiety.

I know she is here but will she be present? Can I reach my Amma today?

By the end of 12th grade, Murali ruled out all other career options. His family was gravely concerned when he only applied to medical school. His options were narrowed.

"My mother worried. 'What if you don't get in? You will go nowhere.'"

That was a long hot summer for Murali in Kakinada. Every day he trekked to the newspaper office where he waited on word via the telegraph. The editor took pity on him. One day as the presses started to roll, faint newspapers began to roll off the end. Pressmen worked to bring the ink into register. A smiling editor walked to Murali and handed him a gray newspaper with faint type on it. And there among the list of names: **R. Murali Krishna.** He had been accepted to medical school at Andhra Medical College in Visakhapatnam. He ran as fast as he could to tell his parents.

"I ran home and hugged my mom, then I ran to my cousins to tell them. It was a great day of celebration."

But then the hard work began.

"My father did not know how we were going to pay. He started writing letters to a few close relatives and some of them did what they could."

A favorite teacher learned of a little-known government scholarship.

"I sent my grades and wrote the essay, but there were so few applicants I didn't even have to take the test. I got it."

His uncle and his Thatha knew the Raja, or king of that district, so it was off to ask for a scholarship. You could not get in to see the king unless you knew someone who knew him.

Murali and his uncle walked to the fort, up the steps to huge doors. They sat in a waiting area. The ceilings seemed as high as the sky. They waited. His uncle gave him strict instructions. Murali was not to speak unless asked a question. Time crept. They sat patiently, quietly. Finally, the doors opened and they walked in to see the king.

Murali bowed his head, palms together in Namasthe. The king stared at him. He talked to the uncle a bit. Stared some more. More silence. The king nodded and they were dismissed.

The Raja granted him 750 rupees per year. And Murali was off to medical school.

Murali was drawn to the medical school. But it was not the teachers or the students or the library that he wanted to see immediately upon arrival. It was a ping pong table that caught the eye of the now 15-year-old Murali.

He arrived on campus, dropped his belongings in his room and ran for the ping pong table. Upper classmen held the paddles and Murali was shut out. Crushed. He knew he could play, his cousins had taught him. He was angry — really angry.

He lay in bed at night seething. *Why won't they let me play?* One sleepless night turned into three. Then he remembered one of Thatha's important teachings.

"All the problems start from within you and all the solutions will emanate from you. It is about how you view the world. I can't

change them, but I can change myself."

So he set out to better his game. He went to the Railway Club and watched players play. He studied their technique and emulated their styles. He went night after night after night. It took two buses to get there. He picked up a frozen Coke to sip on through the evening. Grades started to slip, but he stayed focused on his game.

It took two years before he reached championship level. He reigned as college champion. He finally had earned the respect of his peers.

"Once I realized that solutions come from within, I began to focus. I played for the University and had so much fun doing it. I learned that if I put my mind to it, I can get things done."

Though he had many friends in medical school, he kept the story of his mother close to his heart.

"I shared with one professor. His name was Dr. Raghunathan. I remember being in his office and deciding to take the opportunity to share. He asked, 'Is that one of the reasons why you came to medical school?'"

Murali knew he wanted to be a healer, but the study of psychiatry was still very experimental. They didn't have the medications that are available today.

How will I be able to help my Amma?

Spiritual healing is what happens to us
as we search for the real cause of the pain. The journey
is more important than finding the answer.

CHAPTER TEN

DR. R. MURALI KRISHNA
ON HEALING AND PERSEVERANCE

There is a difference between healing and curing.

We can heal from almost any situation.

But cures can elude us.

There is a simple beauty in that.

When we talk about a cure, we are describing a specific illness or infection that can be managed, removed or taken away. An infection can be eliminated by an antibiotic. A tumor can often be removed and cure the patient. Most illnesses and infections are complicated, and cure rates vary.

Healing is a different story.

If you suffer the death of a loved one, you cannot get that person back. If your child dies, they are gone forever. Cure in that sense is not possible in day-to-day life. That is when healing comes into play. Healing comes from the word "haelan" meaning to heal or be whole. It is to be sound, connected.

When my mother was ill, I felt very disconnected. My sisters and I felt isolated from our neighbors and friends. We did not understand why our house was no longer filled with laughter.

We can disconnect from our families, society and even

spiritually. We no longer feel protected.

The process of healing begins when you try to find options on how to cope. How can you connect to yourself? Your community? Your spirituality?

Short-term denial can actually become part of the healing process. You have to set aside your grief and sadness long enough each day to function. You can intentionally distract yourself. School was a good distraction for me and for my sisters. When we kept busy with schoolwork, we took some of the energy away from our problems.

When tragedy comes into our lives, we tend to focus on the "why?" Why did this happen? Why did my child die? Why did my mom get sick? Why do I have cancer? The why, why, why may never go away.

Sometimes questions have no answers.

Two people can travel the same path and end up with different experiences. Two people can be exposed to the same illness -- one may get it, another will not.

Why?

I wish we had 100-percent answers to the roots of all diseases and suffering, but we do not.

However, healing is an evolutionary process. As we search for "why," we begin to experience healing along the way.

If someone would have come to me in 1972 and explained the reasons for my mother's illness, I would have missed out on my healing journey. I have not given up on finding answers, but I have looked beyond that. It opened up a different part of the world to me that I would not have had a chance to look through.

Had I been an engineer or remained an internist, I would not have seen what I have seen. I would not have learned so much about mental illness and diseases of the brain. Her suffering opened up a window of a spiritual nature. While I was searching for a cause, something that I could measure, feel or touch; I discovered the answers are more intangible.

Spiritual healing is what happens to us as we search for the real cause of the pain. The journey is more important than finding the answer.

We cannot force it. We cannot put a deadline on it.

Some people never move past the "why." They turn bitter. They blame others. They blame God. They blame themselves.

Others turn their suffering into a passion. They define areas of control and put all their energy into something transformative. They turn their negative into a positive.

When I felt ostracized from the ping pong table, my pain was not really about a silly game. It was about feeling disconnected. Life lessons can come in all shapes and sizes – even as small as a ping pong ball.

I knew I could practice and make myself better. It may have been a metaphor for my life. I knew I could not control my mother's illness. But in working so hard at ping pong, I realized there were areas of my life I could control. I found inner strength and perseverance. What started as a ping pong quest transferred to all areas of my life.

I learned I could focus my attention and bring about change. It taught me that I could find resources within myself. If you are not given an opportunity to prove yourself, you will not grow.

Change is growth.

Change is life.

Life is a moving stream. Sometimes we have the delusion that life is settled, not changing. But we are wrong. Some changes are subtle, others are huge. Those are the opportunities for growth. Opportunities for healing.

Learning to accept change is part of life. Some change takes over our lives, like the death of a loved one or the loss of our independence. Change is life.

People that see change as a normal part of life are happier and more successful. They have more awareness of the importance of grasping it and learning to adapt to it. They don't just cope. They develop resources to adapt to change. They acknowledge choices and take action.

The recognition of change is vital to living a healthy and full life.

We must be introspective and look for the options. What choices do I have? In all situations perseverance plays a role. But keep the focus on yourself. If you are expecting others to change, it may never happen. They may not feel the need to change. How can you adapt to the situation so the best of you comes through?

Let life unfold.

"Look for the good in people.
We are more than skin and bones. There is a definite
presence of something extremely powerful,
extremely loving and extremely healing.
But you must go through your own journey
to discover its fullness."

PHOTOS

Early photos of Murali in India are few and far between. But with the help of family, he is able to show a few images of life growing up in India. The photos demonstrate the stark contrast between his early years and where he is today. From dusty parks in India to dining with dignitaries, Murali has led an interesting and varied life.

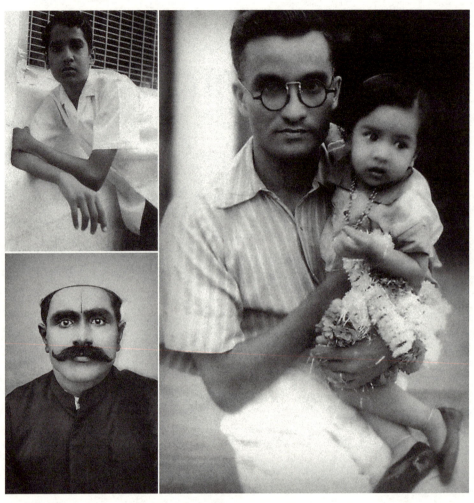

Top left is Murali striking a pose to try out his new camera. Bottom left is Thatha as a tax collector. At right is Murali's father with his sister, Swarajya Lakshmi.

Top, Murali and his sister Rama Devi pose for a photo with his father, R. Swamy, and mother, R. Ranga Rajya Lakshmi. Bottom from left is Thatha in his later years, Murali and Sam.

Top, Murali and Sam during their wedding ceremony. They were not allowed to see one another until the actual ceremony. Below are two group photos of Murali and some of his friends from medical school.

Top, Murali and Sam pose for their official marriage photo which was taken in a studio after their wedding. Below, left is their son, Raja, just a few months old. Bottom right is brother-in-law Gopala Krishna, Murali with nephew Srinivas, and sisters Swarajya Lakshmi and Rama Devi.

Top left is Murali with his nephew Srinivas. Bottom left, is Sam with Vijay and grandson Rohin. At right, the official wedding photo for the family. From left, his father R. Swamy, family nanny Buri, Amma holding nephew Prasad, sisters Rama Devi and Swarajya Lakshmi, nephew Srinivas, Murali and Sam.

Top are Murali and Sam with President George H.W. Bush in Oklahoma City. Bottom left is a photo of the Tri-Board of Health at the State Capitol. Bottom right, Doug Stussi presents Murali with the United Way John Rex Community Builder Award.

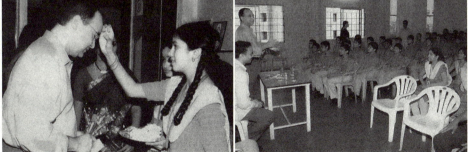

Top, Murali chats with President Bill Clinton during the 10th anniversary of the Oklahoma City bombing of the Alfred P. Murrah Federal Building. Below left is Murali receiving a warm welcome from school students in India. At right, Murali addresses students in class while on a visit to India.

Top left, Murali and Sam don their finest clothes and pause for a quick photo at the inauguration when he was named president of the Oklahoma County Medical Society. At right, the top two photos show friends and dignitaries attending the Bridges to Access Day at the University of Oklahoma College of Medicine. The R. Murali Krishna award is presented annually to an outstanding student who has demonstrated a committment to community service throughout their medical studies. Bottom right is Murali with Gene Barth and Bruce Lawrence at an INTEGRIS Gala.

Top left are attendees and honorees at the Bridges to Access Day. Middle left is Dr. James Claflin presenting the president's gavel to Murali for the Oklahoma County Medical Society. Bottom left is Murali leading the walk for the National Alliance for the Mentally Ill, or NAMI. Top right is Dr. James Caldwell presenting the Dr. Ed Calhoon award for leadership to Murali. Bottom right is Murali presenting the award given in his name to Brandon Geister, fourth-year medical student at OU.

Top left, Murali and Sam's grandchildren Sanjiv, Leela, Anish and Ajay. Bottom left, daughter Bindu shows off her Mehindi before her wedding. It is a tradition in India to decorate the hands and feet. Right is Murali and his family, Bindu, Atul, Leela, Murali, Sam, Raja, Sreele and Sanjiv.

Top left are grandchildren Leela and Rohin playing with cousins Simran and Maya. Bottom left is daughter-in-law Sreele and son Ajay. Top right is beautiful wife, Sam, smelling a bouquet of flowers. Bottom right is Murali and granddaughter Leela.

Top is Murali with family from left, are nephew Krishna Row, niece Ramani, Sam, Murali, Sam's sister Geetha, niece Sheila and son Raja. Bottom left, grandson Sanjiv is welcomed by Sam, Sreele, Raja, Murali, Krishna Dev and Ramani. Bottom right is a portrait of Murali and wife, Sam.

Sam and Murali take the final step
which is to pledge love and sacrifice. They vow to stay loyal
to each other and remain together through good times and bad.
They promise to stay lifelong companions.

CHAPTER ELEVEN

A PRETTY GIRL NAMED SAM

In Murali's last year of medical school, his uncle came to visit unexpectedly.

It was an important visit — one that would forever change his life.

"My uncle came to school and told me the family had found a match for me. I agreed to go to Kakinada and hear them out."

Her name is Syamala Devi Chelikani. "We call her Sam."

Matches were made between two families. Not only the individual, but the family was given very high importance. There was no dating in the traditional sense. Couples at that time were not allowed to talk or even meet before the wedding. All communication was between messengers.

It was not the first match between the two families. Sam and Murali had mutual cousins. The cousins often served as go-betweens during the months leading up to the wedding, sharing bits of enticing information.

"They told me she was always surrounded by friends, that I would have a hard time even getting close to her."

Murali's family strongly encouraged him.

At left is Sam. Murali says this is his favorite photo of his wife.

"I think my father was worried about us getting married sometimes because of the stigma of my mother's illness. I sat down with my parents and my sister and discussed it. My older sister strongly encouraged me to marry Sam. I was not planning on getting married so soon."

Marriage is approached from a practical standpoint in India.

"It is more modern now, but in the olden days it was all about the families. Very practical. Romance comes later. It is more like an aged wine. It gets better and better and better."

Though Murali's family was all in, there was some trepidation on Sam's side. Her grandmother wanted Sam to marry her cousin, which was common at that time.

"She wanted her grandchildren to marry each other, but Sam did not want to."

Eventually the grandmother gave her blessing, and Sam's family approached Murali's uncle and aunt to discuss the match.

"The first move has to be from the girl's family."

The match is made. The wedding is planned.

Weddings are a three-day affair in India. It took place in Sam's hometown of Rajam.

"Hundreds of people come. They travel for days. Everyone who knows you will come to the wedding. I was the first of my classmates to marry, so they all loaded up on a bus to come to the ceremony."

Sam's parents sent out the hand-written invitations.

"You can't send a wedding invitation in print. It would be an insult. You take the time to write them."

The tents are up. And the fun begins. The women are cooking. Smells of vegetables prepared with Indian spices fill the air mixing with sounds of children laughing and playing. It is a time of great celebration.

*Murali catches glimpses of Sam when he can, but they stay
mostly apart until the third day when the actual ceremony takes
place. There is one final task that must be completed before the
couple can officially unite. It is a unique custom on Murali's side
of the family. Generations have come and gone, but the tradition
continues. A member of the Rechi tribe must be satisfied with gifts
before a man of Murali's family can marry. Legend says members
of the Rechi tribe once saved ancestors of Murali's family. From
that time on, the tribe would be repaid with gifts upon the marriage
of all male members of the family.*

*With a curtain dividing them, Murali and Sam sit on the floor
before the Rechi tribal member in a large tent. They are surrounded
by family members as the conversation begins. Gifts of clothes,
money, special shoes are discussed. As the gifts begin to escalate,
Murali's uncle ends the discussion and announces it will resume
the next day.*

"My uncle had a very frank discussion with him that night. By
the next day he seemed to know his limit."

*Festivities resume. The tedious process of painting intricate
detail on the bride's hands, feet and face begins. Gorinta leaves
are soaked and ground to a fine paste. The painting or drawing
procedure is called Mehindi. Sam sits patiently while the bright
reddish-orange ink stains her hands and feet in minute detail. A
smaller design is painted on her face.*

*Murali is less patient as he waits to catch a glance at his
betrothed.*

"She was a beauty. She had beautiful eyes, a wonderful
smile and a good heart. "

*Day three of the festivities finally arrives. It is finally time for
the ceremony. The couple is still not allowed to look directly at
one another. A silk cloth separates them at the beginning of the
ceremony. No affection is shown. As the ceremony proceeds, the silk*

cloth unites the couple with special knots which are tied with sacred thread. It is time for the tradition of the Seven Steps.

Each step represents a vow.

Sam and Murali take the first step: It is a prayer for nourishment and provisions. They ask God to walk beside them so they can work together and always have food.

The second step is a prayer for happiness and health. They pledge to live a healthy life in all aspects including physical, mental and spiritual.

They continue around the fire with step three, which is for wealth and prosperity. They pledge to walk side by side to increase wealth through righteous means.

Step four binds the two families together through mutual trust and loyalty. Murali and Sam pray for noble children from God.

The fifth step is grand in nature. They pray for the welfare of the universe and virtue. They pledge to lead a productive life, to accept children and to take on the responsibility of parenting.

They are united in friendship in the sixth step. It is one of long life, joy and togetherness. They ask God to keep their friendship strong and to give them the maturity to make it lasting. They pledge harmony in their relationship.

Sam and Murali take the final step which is to pledge love and sacrifice. They vow to stay loyal to each other and remain together through good times and bad. They promise to stay lifelong companions.

After the wedding, Murali and Sam spent some time traveling. They went to several temples where they prayed together. And they talked. And they talked. And they talked. They are getting to know one another.

"Sam is a great conversationalist. That was a special bonding time for us. Everything they had told me about her was true."

Still very young, the couple settled in as Murali finished his classes and began working as a general doctor in Sam's hometown of Rajam. The year was filled with one patient after another. He delivered babies, answered his door in the middle of the night and worked through the night when needed. A family doctor cares for the young, the old and all those in between. It is demanding, yet highly rewarding. Murali enjoyed the work, but knew the pace would eventually lead to his own poor health.

"You can't do everything. There is always one more patient to see."

On one rare occasion, Murali and Sam were dining out. Murali felt a thump upside his head and turned to find one of his professors from medical school.

"What are you doing here," the professor asked. "You were selected for the internal medicine residency."

Murali had not known he was selected. After much thought, he and Sam decided he should pursue internal medicine. They knew they could always return to Rajam when the residency was complete.

The internal medicine program was quite rigorous, and Murali knew he would have little time for his family. Sam was pregnant with their first child. She moved back to stay with her parents so they could help with the baby. Murali went back to Vizag so he could concentrate on his studies.

Raja was born Jan. 2, 1972. One of Murali's teachers delivered him.

"Our families asked us how we were going to support a baby. We were only 22 and 21."

The young couple saved every penny and bought a camera to chronicle their young son's life.

"I took hundreds of pictures of Raja. That was a passion for me. He brought such joy to our lives."

Weekdays were for studying; weekends were for family. Murali went from Vizag to Rajam most weekends to see Sam and Raja.

Murali would enter the front door as young Raja toddled over to his open arms. He pointed to Sam as if to introduce Murali to his wife.

"I had some thoughts about closeness. I wanted to give Raja a lot of my time, attention and love -- right from his birth."

After a year and a half of studying internal medicine, Murali still feels the pull of his own Amma. He wants to know what went wrong. He still wants to help her. Mental illness at that time was focused only on the psychotic. There was no counseling. There were only two places in India Murali could have gone to study psychiatry. Both would have required him to learn another language.

I have to learn more for my Amma. There has to be a way I can help.

After researching, Murali found an opportunity in England.

How can I tell Sam I want to move to England? How can I afford to take her and Raja with me?

Murali knew Sam had planned a life for them in Rajam. It was home to her and also close to Thatha's village. Nevertheless, Amma's illness continued to tug at Murali's heart.

"Initially, she did not want to go. But once I shared with her that I wanted to help my mom, she agreed to it. I had to go alone at first. It was 1973. We didn't have enough money for all of us to travel."

It was a lonely time for Murali. He missed his young family. He plowed into his first internal medicine rotation. He found he had a knack for endoscopy and it didn't take long to learn he also had a skill for reading EKGs. He had many options within the medical field. And when it came time to declare his specialty, it was quite a shock to his teachers and mentors.

"They asked me why I wanted to do psychiatry. I asked them, 'Why not?'"

Murali sits in front of a panel of doctors. Stern faces press him for answers.

Why psychiatry? Why not cardiology? Why not gastroenterology? Only doctors who can't do something else go into psychiatry. There is not enough research in the field? You will be disappointed.

Murali still does not share his reasons.

"I didn't have the courage to share the story of my mom. There was still too much stigma. I didn't want them to think I was going into it to solve my own problems or my mom's problems. It took weeks before they gave their approval."

Unbeknownst to Murali, his young bride was back home trying to think of a way to unite her family. She desperately wanted to get to England and put her little family back under one roof.

Sam gingerly removed her ankle ornaments and carried them to her father-in-law. They had been given to her by her family, but the need to have her family together was paramount over sentimentality.

Murali's father sold the jewelry and sent mother and child to England.

Challenges are what make us stronger.
When challenged, introspective people will find strength
from their inner core. You can find your potential
during challenging times.

CHAPTER TWELVE

DR. R. MURALI KRISHNA
ON LOVE AND MARRIAGE

How can two people who have never met expect to have a long and happy marriage?

Commitment.

When two people find each other through whatever means, they will not last without commitment.

I am often asked about my arranged marriage to my wife, Sam. Can I tell you that we were instantly madly in love with each other? No. But we were infatuated with one another. And I can tell you our love has evolved through the years, and we have a genuine love. I simply adore my wife. We have been together 43 years. She is the light of my life.

Committed relationships work.

The strongest couples know and live by five components of love and commitment:

1. They know that love evolves, and they nurture it.
2. They have a common purpose.
3. They are willing to maintain their individuality and still know when to put their spouse first. Their relationship is a priority.
4. They accept their spouse unconditionally.
5. They are truly grateful for each other.

LOVE EVOLVES

God has created stages of love in a beautiful sequence. If you ask young people in their teens or early 20s, they may talk about love in terms of physical beauty and sex. As couples age, they will begin to focus on common interests. As you go deeper and deeper, they will find a common passion both in life and for each other. The ultimate love is a spiritual union. It is so strong that it cannot be separated by age, illness, trauma, loss or even death. That kind of union is what keeps us believing in something beyond our presence here on earth. That is the ultimate level of love.

But that takes nurturing.

Every couple has to find a reasonable way of nurturing their relationship. Know when to give and when to take. Learn to look through the other person's eyes. Learn to listen.

Every couple will be faced with ups and downs. Careers, children, illness, financial troubles and a myriad of other things can create challenges. All those challenges can lead the couple to put their marriage on the back burner. But a solid foundation will keep the marriage strong through the challenges. Love is essential, and it will reinvigorate itself when there is understanding and communication.

The foundation is solid trust and commitment.

A COMMON PURPOSE

Strong couples share passion and a common purpose. They know what gives meaning to their lives. It might be their children or grandchildren. It might be their church or an activity like gardening, hiking or fishing. It helps to be involved within the community. We all need connectedness not only with each other, but with the world around us. Most healthy people have a strong passion for something. Find a common passion. Seek it out.

A SENSE OF PRIORITY

Couples with strong and open communication will weather the barrage of peaks and valleys that life hurls their way. They listen to one another and realize when they must put their spouse first. They consciously work at supporting one another. Each person must maintain a sense of individuality, but there are times for sacrifice as well. You must be willing to share your hopes and dreams with one another and show your support. Every couple will disagree, but you must learn to express yourself without alienating the other person.

Couples need to know when they are in trouble. They may need to seek outside counsel to help them navigate through an issue. And every couple will have issues.

Challenges are what make us stronger. When challenged, introspective people will find strength from their inner core. You can find your potential during challenging times.

Life can offer both calm seas and tidal waves. We have to learn to expect troubles --prepare for them, deal with them and become stronger.

UNCONDITIONAL LOVE

Couples must love each other unconditionally and accept each other as they are.

Very rarely does another human being meet our expectations. We are not divine beings. We are human. We are imperfect.

Humans can be emotionally messy. Sometimes spouses look

to one another to fill a void they have from within. No one can fill a void for you. People who marry many times may be trying to fill their own spiritual void. That kind of void can never be filled by another human being. Spirituality and true happiness come only from within.

If a spouse seeks connection with someone else outside of the marriage, they are searching for something that they will not find. If it is sex, it will not feed their spiritual longing. Sex is largely in the mind. When it comes down to it, sex is the same act over and over and over. The act hasn't changed in millions of years. Of course there are variations of it, but it is fleeting. It is short-term gratification. A person who is insecure can be easily swayed by someone from outside the marriage. They think they must be important or special to deserve the focused attention. But it will not last. They will repeat the process until they realize their emptiness and insecurity comes from within. Some couples will throw away their whole marriage over sex. They will say, "I can't sleep with you anymore." There is so much more to a relationship than sex.

GRATITUDE

Sometimes when a spouse dies, the surviving spouse realizes how much they miss them and they have regrets about not showing greater appreciation for them when they were still living. If we could only feel even a small part of that when the other person is still here, it would make the relationship so much better. If we have a sense of gratitude for our spouse, we will interact with them more positively. You will not take them for granted. Learn to appreciate their energy, their passion, their partnership with you. Be present in your relationship. Take the time to savor simple moments together. We all have a return ticket; your time together will come to an end.

LAUGHTER

If there were a sixth component to a committed marriage, it would have to be laughter. Having a sense of humor makes life more enjoyable. If you and your spouse can find humor in the simple aspects of life, your journey together will be smoother and brighter. Laughter can take the stress out of many situations.

Enjoy the ride.

I was learning so much.
It was a most fulfilling time. I learned beyond
what a text book could teach me.

CHAPTER THIRTEEN

WHERE IS OKLAHOMA?

The young family settled into residency at New Cross Hospital in Wolverhampton, England, about 100 miles from London. They lived in small quarters on the large campus and enjoyed meals in the hospital cafeteria. Everything was provided in their small apartment. Murali worked long hours. Sam focused on Raja.

Murali was finally looking into the faces of patients just like Amma.

"What I learned there at least gave her a few years of stability. I learned about lithium and other drugs used for thought and mood disorders. Psycho pharmacology was very strong in England. I worked through her doctor and it provided some of the most stable periods of her life."

Murali was learning about his mother's illness, and Sam and Raja were content living on the campus.

It all started to change when Murali presented an article to the journal club at the hospital. Written by Dr. Jay Shurley, the article focused on sensory deprivation.

Dr. Shurley lived in Oklahoma City.

A letter to Dr. Shurley from Murali led to more letters and then an invitation to come to Oklahoma City for another residency program.

At left, Murali and Sam with son Raja in England.

"I applied to five places in the U.S. and one of them was the University of Oklahoma. I was accepted to all five."

It was a phone call from Dr. Agustín Lopez that finalized the plan. But that phone call was not for Murali.

Murali returned home one evening to find that Sam had spent time on the phone with Dr. Lopez.

"She said, 'We are going to Oklahoma.' We didn't even know where it was exactly."

He recalled speaking to telephone operators who would sing "Oklahoma" to him.

"I didn't know anything about that song. I wondered why they were singing. I also remember them asking me why I was going there. One operator said, 'Oklahoma? Do you know they call petrol 'gas' there?'"

He was met with more surprises at the Embassy when he went to apply for a visa.

"The lady said to me, 'Young man, do you want to go as a visitor or an immigrant?' I told her I was going there to become a citizen -- a doctor in the U.S. She told me it would take one to two years to get that done. So I called and told them in Oklahoma it would be one to two years before I could come. I did not want to go as a visitor; I wanted to become a citizen."

Murali's early exposure to the U.S. came from missionaries, Peace Corps workers and stories from his Thatha.

"The U.S. was the shining city on the hill for me."

Drs. Lopez and Shurley told him not to worry. They were going to talk with Dr. Charlie Smith.

"They said, 'He knows everybody.' All I knew was that two men named Bellmon and Bartlett intervened and that I had three green cards within a matter of weeks."

He later learned it was United States Senators Henry Bellmon and Dewey Bartlett.

At 11 p.m. on March 29, 1975, Murali, Sam and Raja arrived at Will Rogers World Airport in Oklahoma City.

"Dr. Lopez and his wife picked us up at the airport and took us to their home. We had a wonderful dinner of Cuban food. It was very late before we got to the hotel. Dr. Lopez picked me up at 7 a.m. to go to the hospital. For the next few weeks, he drove me there each morning. And he would wait until I finished and take me home. I was floored by all the affection we were shown."

It was a time of great adventure — a new country, no car, no household necessities and no family. But the list of friends was growing daily.

They lived in the Park Manor Apartments on 63rd Street.

"It was especially hard for Sam. She had to walk in the beginning. She walked across May Avenue to take Raja to pre-school each day. We only made $500 a month, but we had a lot of joy."

Dining out was rare, but when they did eat out it was at Dairy Queen or occasionally Monterrey House, the Mexican restaurant on May Avenue.

Murali realized he could take a second job moonlighting at the Coyne Campbell Hospital in Spencer. Thus began the cycle of working long hours. Murali was asked at OU if he wanted to consider child psychiatry. It would mean more training.

"At that point, Sam asked me, 'When are you going to stop training and start making money? It is time.' She was right. I loved learning, but it was time to start working and getting a salary we could live on."

The little family of three grew to four on Sept. 29, 1977 when Hema Bindu Krishna was born.

"It was odd for Sam. When our daughter was born, Sam only had one friend with her at the hospital. In India, new moms are surrounded by family and friends. But Sam managed and we had our beautiful daughter, Bindu. It was a time of great joy."

By now, Murali had many close mentors in his life, including Dr. Povl Tousseing, Drs. Lopez and Shurley, Dr. Gordon Deckert and Dr. Charlie Smith. Smith asked Murali to work with him and Dr. Bob Outlaw in private practice. They had offices at 12th Street and Shartel with privileges at Saint Anthony Hospital. Murali would see patients through the day then go to the hospital in the evening for consultations.

He also continued to consult with his mother's doctors in India, until her death in the early 80s. Medical treatment brought her some relief in her later days.

The years of long days and exhausting demands finally caught up to the young doctor in the mid '80s.

After a 16-hour day at the hospital, Murali came home after midnight. Soon after he arrived, Sam found him collapsed in the bathroom. He was rushed into surgery to remove his appendix.

"It was on the last layer, almost bursting. I think I was just too busy to notice the pain. I knew it was time to start listening to some of my own advice. I greatly needed balance in my life. That's when I started playing tennis again. In India I didn't have enough money to play, and in the U.S. I didn't have enough time."

He continued to grow his private practice. He expanded his responsibilities at Saints. He was first vice chair, then chair of the Psychiatry Department. In 1994, he was elected unanimously as Chief of Staff for Saint Anthony Hospital. He was the first psychiatrist ever appointed to the post.

And the balancing act continued. In the '90s, he and Raja would go to the hospital early on Saturday mornings. Raja would be anxious for his dad to wrap up rounds so they could go to Norman and watch OU play football. The father-son duo, thousands of miles from India, had become Sooners.

Most days, Murali was gone from early in the morning until late at night. Nevertheless, Bindu waited up for her father to read her a story.

"I would read to her then sneak slowly out of the room. I would hear her say, 'Daddy, I am not sleepy yet,' and I would have to read her another one. I could never spend as much time as I wanted to spend. It was just work, work, work."

Balance is something Murali would chase for many years. Much like his pursuit to help his mother, spending more time with his family was forever near his heart.

How can I help all the people who need me? How can I be there for Sam, Raja and Bindu?

The mental health program at Saints was expanding. Dick Mooney was the administrator.

"I also got to know the nuns. I have such respect for Dick Mooney and the sisters. We had a beautiful experience working together."

One of the outcomes was the creation of the SHARE program. It was a day program based on a rehabilitative environment. Murali worked diligently with his ever-present assistant Susie Waugh, R.N. Susie served as the program coordinator. She was quoted in a Share newsletter saying, "Our greatest strengths are our exceptionally qualified staff, our size which allows us to be flexible, and our emphasis on education and prevention. It feels good to work at something you believe in, and I believe in Share."

"I have the sheer belief that if you do the right thing, good things will happen. We worked hard to create this program and it was successful," said Murali. "Susie has worked with me since 1978."

As the young psychiatrist was helping his patients, they were helping him as well.

"I was learning so much. It was a most fulfilling time. I learned beyond what a text book could teach me."

But the one lesson he still needed to learn was beyond his grasp.

Balance.

Start slowly in exploring how
to reapportion your life. Make changes gradually,
but deliberately. Start living your life with intent. Be deliberate
in how you choose to spend your day.

CHAPTER FOURTEEN

DR. R. MURALI KRISHNA
ON EMOTIONAL, PHYSICAL AND SPIRITUAL BALANCE

Balance.

So desired, yet so elusive.

Balance eludes us because we all think we are capable
of doing more than we can realistically accomplish. We feel
we are invincible. Balance, we tend to think, is what others
need. Too many of us fall into the trap of thinking we can do
anything and everything -- all at once.

For me, it took emergency surgery to get my attention.
That made me pause. While I was home recuperating from the
appendectomy, I went for a walk with my daughter, Bindu.
As we strolled slowly along admiring nature and flowers, she
looked up at me and said, "Daddy, I wish you could be sick for a
little bit longer." I knew what she really meant was, "Daddy, I
wish you would spend more time with me."

That statement was haunting for me.

I had allowed my career to dominate every aspect of my
life. I allowed my passion to devour me. I felt invincible and
thought I could go on at that pace forever.

I didn't stop to ask myself what the endpoint was. What was

my goal? I was just blindly following my heart and my passion. Without an illness, I would not have paused. It should not take an illness for us to stop and evaluate our lives.

Where are we going? What is our goal? Why?

We all have a finite amount of resources. We only have so much energy. We can only tolerate a certain amount of intensity before our cup overflows. If we forego fun and joy, we will eventually begin to have regrets and resentments. Along with that comes physical symptoms such as cardiovascular, gastrointestinal and immune system problems. The symptoms of burnout and overload closely resemble the symptoms of depression.

When you think you are performing on all cylinders, you might be fooling yourself. Without balance in your life, the quality of your work will eventually suffer.

When I examined my life, I realized I had abandoned many things I enjoyed doing as a child. When I was young, I read books for enjoyment and to expand my mind. I had cast those aside for medical studies and information on mental illness. I had abandoned travel and adventure. So Sam and I loaded the kids in our silver Volvo station wagon and took vacations. Even with two kids fighting in the backseat, you can find a sense of wonder and enjoyment.

I also knew I had to spend more time in prayer. In short, I started to listen to what I had been telling my patients.

I discovered that the creative part of my life started to return. I realized my entire focus was on sick care. I was helping patients one at a time. I knew I needed a paradigm shift so I could help society as a whole.

Life is filled with teachable moments. I reapportioned my life and my time.

When you take an inventory of how you spend your time,

you may find that you feel as if you are the only one who can accomplish a certain task or special part of your job. But you must realize that if you were the only person on earth to get the job done, then God would have given you magical powers.

Stop. Acknowledge your finite resources.

Every person on this earth can find balance in life. Here are some questions to ask yourself in exploring your own balance.

1. Do you feel you are accomplishing in your life what you want to accomplish?
2. Are you neglecting certain areas of your life?
3. Do you have inner peace?
4. Are you wondering why you do what you do?
5. Is there something lacking in your life?
6. Are you getting any signals from your mind, body or spirit that you need to listen to?
7. Are you going in the right direction?
8. Are you doing everything you can, but still feel dissatisfied?
9. Is the creative, vibrant, energetic aspect of you alive and thriving? Or has it shut down?
10. Are you savoring each moment as it unfolds in your life?
11. Are you having successes that have ceased to give you fulfillment or inner satisfaction?
12. Is the money and good reputation enough for you?
13. Are you postponing dreams to a later date?
14. Do you feel overwhelmed?
15. Are you the captain of your own life?
16. Is your life out of control?
17. Do you feel you have choices and options?

Ask yourself these questions honestly. Then sit down and

take stock of your life. Inventory your time.

Do you have enough joy in your life? Do you take time to play? To pray?

Creativity and spirituality go hand in hand. Reaching the creative part of our mind is attaining a level of spirituality. One is part of the other. It takes time to let our minds wander and be creative.

Start slowly in exploring how to reapportion your life. Make changes gradually, but deliberately. Start living your life with intent. Be deliberate in how you choose to spend your day.

But it's important to remember that there is far more to **balance** than simply managing your time.

Be present.

If you reapportion your time but your mind is elsewhere, you are still out of balance. You have to learn to live in the moment. We see the sun set every day, but do we really see it? Do we pause and become one with it. Do we savor it?

We all have moments in life when we feel that life is great. Something magical happens when we immerse ourselves in what we are doing and thinking right at this moment.

Even time at work can become more balanced. Recognize your role in the world. We all contribute to humanity. No matter what your job is, think about how you connect. For example, if you pour coffee, stop for a moment and think about the larger picture. Think about the farmer who toiled under the sun to grow the coffee beans. Think about how those beans were processed and delivered from the fields to the distribution centers to the restaurants and stores. Think about the customer who is able to enjoy one of God's simple creations.

Everything in life connects.

We want to thrive, not just survive.

A balanced person is an adaptable person. The sign of a

truly balanced person is one who can handle what the world throws his or her way. Even from a physical standpoint, a person who is balanced can better fight off illness and disease.

Balance in itself is a journey. As we travel through life, we have to tweak our priorities.

It is a constant process of deliberate and conscious adjustment.

God give us strength to help these people.

CHAPTER FIFTEEN

TERROR IN MY CITY

It was April 19, 1995.

Murali started his day with a tennis match.

Like many Oklahomans, he was going about his business —
tennis, shower, packing a suitcase for a flight later that day.
As chief of staff, he had planned a retreat to Houston for the
leadership of Saint Anthony Hospital.

Murali didn't know Timothy McVeigh was threading a Ryder
truck slowly through traffic in downtown Oklahoma City. He
didn't know evil was descending upon his city. He didn't know
a bomb was about to explode, forever altering the course of so
many lives.

And end the lives of 168 people, including 19 children at a
day-care center.

He didn't know his world would change that day. No one did.

It was 9:02 a.m.

"I heard and felt the loud boom. Sam's parents were here
visiting. My father-in-law walked outside to see if he could see
anything. We did not know what it was. But a few minutes
later the hospital called and said there had been an explosion."

Who? What? Where? When? WHY? All questions, no
answers.

*At left, a bomb rips away most of the Alfred P. Murrah Federal Building in Okla-
homa City. (Photo used with permission, The Oklahoman.)*

He first went to the scene of the Alfred P. Murrah Federal Building. The homemade truck bomb had sheared away half the building.

People were running. Not running away from the building, but running toward it.

"You normally see people fleeing a scene like that, but that was not the case. The police had a hard time keeping people out. They would sneak back in and try to help."

Chaos.

Terror.

It became clear to Murali that he was most needed at the hospital. Being the closest hospital, St. Anthony would soon be overrun with patients.

Within minutes, the halls filled with nurses, staff members and doctors of every specialty. They all showed up. And so did the injured.

The streets around St. Anthony were filled with throngs of people. The injured were streaming in and their injuries were severe. Deep cuts, severed arteries, missing eyes, burns – injuries more in line with a war zone than the streets of a Midwestern state capital.

How could this happen? Why? Murali prayed throughout the day.

"God give us strength to help these people."

Patients. More patients.

The seasoned psychiatrist was taking note of what he would later define as a very strange phenomenon.

"People were not arguing and making demands. Many of the patients were offering to let others go before them. It was strangely quiet."

Murali knows that people in pain often panic, but that was not the case on that sunny April morning.

"Everyone had a job to do and they were doing it."

As chief of staff, Murali began getting phone calls from other doctors wanting to help. Dr. Shurley showed up and added a sense of calmness to the situation for Murali. He had seen mass injuries in war. He and Murali discussed the emotional devastation that would hold victims in a vice-like grip for days, weeks and even years to come. It would spread beyond victims to family members, friends and people around the world. The stranglehold of terror descended upon the United States when people everywhere came to the realization that they could wake up one day, go to work and never return to their families. They could be sitting in an office one moment and descend into a mass of dust and steel the next.

Terror.

Dr. Krishna and his team set up a room in the basement of the behavioral health area of the hospital to allow victims and their families a place to share, a place to decompress.

"They just needed to share with one another. There was so much anxiety."

Rescue soon turned to recovery. But what happened in Oklahoma City was nothing short of a miracle.

Every need was met for the rescue and recovery workers. A steady stream of volunteers kept the makeshift camp running smoothly. Meals were cooked, clothes were cleaned, beds were made. Even haircuts were offered. Workers came from across the country to painstakingly remove debris bit by bit. It was the largest crime scene in U.S. history.

The collective soul of Oklahoma was battered. But it would rise.

"I have seen it with my own eyes. We may be obese, have heart problems and dental problems, but Oklahomans are the kindest people on earth. We are Oklahomans for the rest of our lives. We will be very much a part of society here for generations to come. I have seen acts of kindness, acts of compassion – nowhere could top it."

The first three days were a blur for Murali -- for all Oklahomans. Days began before sunrise and lasted into the next day. The media was hungry for information. Interview requests were mounting. Murali was interviewed by networks and media outlets from all over the world. His family and friends in India read about him and followed the news coverage. Sam fielded calls from them as Murali spent hours upon hours at the hospital.

At the end of the third night, Murali made his way slowly to his car on the first level of the parking garage. Another doctor approached him and asked a simple question.

"He said to me, 'Murali, how do you do it? I know you are tired and you want to go home, but I want to ask you a question. What makes you so good?' I was taken aback. I told him I don't know how good I am, lots of people I know work really hard too."

The doctor pressed further.

"He said, 'Murali, people trust you, they like you. What makes you different? I want you to think about it.' I laughed it off and got in my car."

He was weary from the day, but it was nice to get a compliment. But the question lingered for a bit.

"I thought maybe I am just lucky with opportunity; maybe I had good mentors. I didn't really know."

He drove home, walked inside and had his dinner. Sam always keeps his dinner no matter how late he stays at the hospital. Exhausted from a long day, he went to bed and fell fast asleep.

Then his eyes popped open. Awake.

"I just woke up all of a sudden. It was like a light bulb went on. I realized it was not because of my education or my mentors or my intelligence. I knew people who had better education and were smarter than me. The reason I succeeded was because of my mother. I had learned to connect to the pain and distress of others. I had genuine empathy of the heart."

It was as if Amma's suffering somehow made sense now. Murali realized he had grown into the doctor he was at that moment because of his mother's illness — her sacrifice.

The world started to change for Murali. He was previously on a path to finish out his career in a decade or two, retire comfortably and enjoy his golden years. But the spirit of Oklahomans, the spirit displayed by mankind in the wake of despicable acts of terror, grabbed Murali on a very deep level and pushed him. It pushed him to find new ways of helping Oklahomans. It pushed him to do more. It pushed him to be vibrant.

It pushed him to pray to God every day.

"God, please use me up before you take me."

Resilient people are everyday people
who rise to the occasion when faced with a challenge,
change or adversity. We all have the capability to be resilient
and do extraordinary things.

CHAPTER SIXTEEN

DR. R. MURALI KRISHNA ON THE GOODNESS OF HUMANITY AND RESILIENCY

Barriers.

We are separated by many barriers. Busy lives. Self-absorption. Daily routines.

Barriers of race. Barriers of religion and politics.

But when tragedy strikes, we reach across those barriers. We connect with each other. Man to man. Spirit to spirit.

That is the true nature of humanity.

At our core, we are nurturing, caring human beings. We have the ability to put our own needs, comforts and concerns on the back burner. We can reach out to another human being and help. The suffering human who needs help takes priority over everything else.

That's when the barriers are broken. That's when we are at our best.

Someday you may be called upon to pull someone from a crumbled building. Or it may be something as simple as carrying your neighbor's groceries into the house.

Acts of kindness cross barriers. They tap into our inner hero.

FROM THE DARKNESS

After the Oklahoma City bombing, the range of raw emotions within our community was palpable. Anger was strong. Anger toward the bombers. Anger over our shattered innocence. Anger toward God. Why us? Why here? Why now? Why would God let this happen?

When something of value is taken from you, it is natural to ask difficult and challenging questions. Being angry with our Creator is normal. If you didn't believe in Him, you couldn't be angry with Him. It is like being angry with a parent. We have the expectation that we will be taken care of because we are loved. Many people believe God shields us from pain. But no one will be shielded from all pain. Every life experiences pain and loss – usually multiple times.

What God gives us is strength to handle our pain. With God's help, we **can** cope. We can overcome.

The human spirit is resilient.

We can all find resiliency within ourselves. Resiliency is the transformative process in life that changes the dark coal of adversity into a brilliant clear diamond of strength. It is the force that energizes us to grow through adversity or change by discovering our own resources, abilities and strengths.

It is a process that we all possess. Resiliency comes to us in varying degrees at different times of our life. If we look back at our lives, we can find pain and obstacles that seemed insurmountable at the time. For example, a grieving widow may see little reason to go on. But as time passes, little by little, she gains strength.

The resiliency of the human spirit is a beautiful sight to behold. People visibly transform when they make the decision to go on – to keep living. They choose life. For some people, the decision is made quickly. For others, it may take months. There is no timetable or deadline – it varies by the individual.

Resilient people are generally optimistic and seek out joy in even small things. They notice the bluebird or the laughing child. They not only notice small things, they look for them.

The resilient have humility and hope. They look for things to be grateful for and make every attempt to connect with others. They nurture relationships and seek out a network of support. If people are experiencing a loss of death or divorce, they often build a network of friends with whom to share their ups and downs. Don't be afraid to venture out. Support groups can open your mind to new approaches and ideas. You don't always have to share your own feelings in a support group. Just go and listen until you are ready to share.

People who are resilient do not dwell on what others think of them. They give themselves permission to find their own way on their own time. They have self-respect. Self acceptance.

The resilient fundamentally know they need to take care of themselves. They make it a point to exercise and eat healthy. They choose how and where to direct their energy. It is important to make conscious decisions about your health and well-being.

One of the most important aspects of resiliency is to practice patience. Be patient with yourself. During times of great challenge, it is important to tolerate a degree of uncertainty. You may not have all the answers that you are looking for, but you can still have faith that your journey will improve with time. Even the greatest of sorrows loses energy over the course of time.

LEARNING THE ART OF SELF-TALK CAN HELP WITH NEGATIVE THOUGHTS

Recognize the negative thought and make a decision to stop it. Distract yourself or redirect your energy. Practice removing yourself from the negativity. Detach and disengage. Write and share with others. It is important to take steps and be proactive. Go for a walk or do something with your hands. Science has shown us that working with your hands can ease your stress level.

Resilient people are everyday people who rise to the occasion when faced with a challenge, change or adversity. We all have the capability to be resilient and do extraordinary things.

I saw Oklahomans rise beyond their abilities to help their fellow man after the bombing. They discovered a purpose greater than themselves.

They reached across the barriers we face every day and placed their hand in the hand of someone in need. This is the goodness of humanity. We are at our best when we reach out to someone in need.

Oklahoma walked through dark days in April of 1995. We cried together. Our collective spirit was hurting. But we joined hands and are now stronger as a community. When we go beyond healing and rise to new levels, we become vibrant.

I am proud to call Oklahoma City my home.

*We try to help them to learn different ways of looking
at things. They learn different reactions and different behaviors.
We give them tools to quiet the mind.*

CHAPTER SEVENTEEN

A CAREER EVOLVES

More.

Murali simply wanted to do more.

His realization and acknowledgement of his mother's impact on his life tugged at his heart and spirit.

"I was moved to honor her memory. I started sharing my story with others. "

Murali did not know where his path would lead him, but he knew it could involve change.

"I wanted to create more things for Oklahomans that they didn't have. I wanted to create something longer lasting, more permanent. I wanted to impact more lives."

He shared these thoughts with a friend, James L. Hall, Jr., a local attorney. Hall and Murali had discussions about stress management. Hall expressed interest for having a resource center in Oklahoma for the mind-body connection. Hall had done legal work for Baptist Medical Center. He was aware that INTEGRIS Health was being formed and knew there could be possibilities for Murali. But what? The discussions began to take shape. The seed had been planted and Murali knew change was in his future.

But change can bring pain. Saint Anthony Hospital had been

At left, Murali applauds at a local event in Oklahoma City. (Photo used with permission, The Oklahoman.)

his home for 17 years.

"I had never been any place that long. We had a great relationship. We had nurtured each other. It was home."

Hall was president of a national association for health care attorneys, a graduate of Harvard. He had a national stage, and brought the Reverend Bill Carpenter, director of pastoral care at Baptist, into the conversation. At the same time, Murali was discussing the connection between mind and body with Dr. Bill Hawley, a well-known cardiac surgeon. Hawley invited Murali and Sam to his ranch for a discussion with Stanley Hupfeld, chief administrator of the now-forming INTEGRIS Health.

"He asked me to come, sit down and talk about my dreams."

Murali didn't know exactly what he wanted, but he knew it involved the mind, body and spirit. Hupfeld wanted him to create INTEGRIS Mental Health. Murali was up for the challenge, but there were still hurdles to jump.

Hupfeld gave Murali the opportunity to present his mental health concepts to the INTEGRIS staff. It was overwhelmingly accepted by all those in attendance.

"They took a chance on me. What I was bringing was really pie in the sky."

While it was hard for Murali to leave Saints – "especially the doctors and the sisters" -- he wouldn't even consider leaving his practice and the doctors with whom he had worked side by side.

"Surprisingly, Drs. Charlie Smith and Bob Outlaw embraced it."

The final agreement was reached after the whole group met for what was almost a five-hour dinner. Dr. John Andrus, Dr. Twyla Smith and all the others agreed to follow Murali to INTEGRIS Mental Health.

The next step focused on the mind, body, spirit connection.

"Jim Hall and I talked and talked about the mind, body, spirit connection. He brought the people together to make it happen. When he died of cancer, I wanted to name it the James L. Hall Jr. Center for Mind, Body and Spirit. I wanted him to be remembered for his efforts."

The website best describes its mission: *"The INTEGRIS James L. Hall Jr. Center for Mind, Body and Spirit is working to create a more compassionate, open-minded and effective model of health care and health education. This model addresses not just the physical dimensions of health and illness, but the mental, emotional, social and spiritual dimensions as well. It is grounded in a conviction that all of us have a great and largely untapped capacity to understand ourselves, to improve our own health and well-being, and to help one another."*

It provides services in the areas of training, education, workshops and a media center with more than 2,000 books, journals and videos available to the public. The center has hosted a plethora of speakers, including Deepak Chopra, Rob Lowe and more.

"The center strives to educate people on the powers of the mind."

Initially there were skeptics.

"Doctors would say to me, 'Why are you getting mixed up in that Shirley MacLaine-out-on-a-limb type stuff? But once they heard me out, I could convince them."

Murali knew the only way to convince the medical community was through science.

"I spoke at a dinner one time. When dinner ran late and the crowd started getting stressed, I pointed out to them that their chance of a heart attack just went up 230 percent. Anger increases your chances by that much. They had asked me to speak for 20 minutes, but they kept me more than an hour asking questions.

"I shared with them that I used to have panic attacks as a teen. I learned to calm myself. Through trial and error, I learned to meditate and control it. I have taught many patients the same technique. At the time, we didn't know the brain can be changed. But it can be altered by the experiences we give it."

Murali knows that depression and anxiety affect every part of the body.

"In science, we know the telomeres inside our chromosomes shorten and cause aging. In depression, the telomeres shorten faster. You can physically see people age with depression."

The mind, body, spirit center was one of many developments launched by INTEGRIS Mental Health. Another program dear to Murali's heart is Decisions, a day-hospital program. Often, patients do not need severe inpatient treatment, but they still need intensive treatment. The Decisions program brings patients together for a two- to four-week session that runs from morning until late afternoon. They spend time in both individual and group counseling. Their medication is regulated and they focus on learning skills to stabilize their life. The Decisions programs treat depression, post-traumatic stress disorder, anxiety and other mental health problems. It also added an adolescent program and chemical dependency to its list of offerings.

"We get people of all types. We have professionals, executives, mothers, fathers – everyone you can think of. They share a common connection and work well in a group setting. An important aspect of this treatment is to identify the stress triggers and the dysfunctional thinking in feelings and relationships. We try to help them to learn different ways of looking at things. They learn different reactions and different behaviors. We give them tools to quiet the mind.

"Nutrition plays a strong role too. We teach them that what they put into their bodies plays a role in their emotional health."

The move to INTEGRIS has been fruitful for Murali.

"They have given me deep roots and a connection to more people. All my roles have been to further my mission. I didn't need to take on all the positions of responsibility like the County Medical Board, but I saw them as a way to further my cause. Eventually people stopped seeing me as a brown man with an accent.

"They see me as a man who is passionate about mental illness and emotional wellness."

When we embrace and accept
that every life is finite, we start to see life through new eyes.
The value of your life goes up dramatically when you
acknowledge that it is fleeting.

CHAPTER EIGHTEEN

DR. R. MURALI KRISHNA
ON CONNECTEDNESS: GIVING MEANING TO LIFE

Life is lived to its fullest when we connect with one another. Connectedness.

If we can strip away all the trappings of life and reach our inner spirit, we can connect with others at the same level.

That is what happens in a tragedy. Everything is stripped away. We reach out to each other. We touch each other at a very deep level -- a spiritual level. That's humanity as it should be.

If we could capture the love and compassion that flows during times of crisis and bottle it up, our world would be a better place.

When people unite around a common event – even if that event is a tragedy -- they will grow. They will grow as individuals and they will grow as a community. They will heal. They will connect.

Connecting begins when we accept our mortality. When we embrace and accept that every life is finite, we start to see life through new eyes. The value of your life goes up dramatically when you acknowledge that it is fleeting.

Many people live their day-to-day lives focusing on the

temporary aspects of life, taking comfort in their sensory experiences. They like their house, their car and their clothes.

But all aspects of your life are temporary.

And none of those sensory perceptions changes your spirit. You have the same spirit you were born with -- the same soul. The essence of who you are has never changed. Life experiences may alter how you perceive things, but **you** are still **you.**

So as you feel, hear, smell, and taste, ask yourself this: "Who is it that is experiencing this sensation? Who is the person with dreams? Feelings? Talents?

"Who is the real me?"

As scientists, we can determine all physiological functions of the body. But at some point, the scientific pathway to enlightenment stops. From a functional perspective, we know how we see, taste or feel. We know that nerves are stimulated and send signals. But all science ends there. It doesn't answer the fundamental question. Who is receiving the signal? Science can't take us beyond the question we should be asking ourselves:

"Who is the real me?"

And how will I connect?

REACHING OUT

We can connect with our fellow man in many ways – even in the absence of trauma. We can reach out to the sick, to those struggling or to those in mourning. The hurting are always among us.

Look for the divine in others and acknowledge the sacredness of your own purpose. Know that you can impact another human being.

You have the potential to connect.

If you can't find the words, just sit by a friend who is in pain. Your presence is often blessing enough.

You can reach out to a community as well. It might be your church or your neighborhood. What is important is that you dedicate energy and focus to the task.

If you want to start at the most basic level, give someone a smile. Even the smallest actions can make a difference. Don't postpone your good works. Writing a check at the end of the year might help you with your taxes, but an investment of your time throughout the year will give you better emotional return.

BE FILLED WITH WONDER

Giving to others can be fulfilling, but don't forget to give to yourself. One of the greatest gifts you can give yourself is a sense of wonder. Be curious. Learn to ask why. If we live our lives focusing on only what we can see on the surface, we will deprive ourselves of deeper meaning.

Go ahead, dig deeper.

The brightest minds throughout history come from those who continued to ask the most basic question:

"Why?"

They looked for connections where they didn't exist before. Don't fear the unknown. Be curious. What lies beyond what we can see?

Different religions have differing viewpoints. But if we acknowledge our fellow man as a spiritual being, there would be no room for animosity – and certainly no room for fighting wars over religion.

Focusing on our spirit elevates us to a higher level. We have to be willing to leave our comfort zones and connect with our spirit and the spirit of others.

Be courageous. Reach higher. Reach for truth. Live with vibrance.

Wonder about your world and what lies beyond it.

I just knew I had a passion. As human beings,
we all have an inner deep longing to connect and help others.
If we can uncover it, it will come out. I've yet to see it fail.
It is inherent in each of us.

CHAPTER NINETEEN

HELPING THE HURTING

When Murali crosses one finish line, he looks for another. He continues to raise the bar.

When he says he wants God to use him up before he dies, he means it. One project begets another and yet another. Titles and accomplishments are fleeting.

"What good is a title or accolade if you cannot do something good with it? You are given talents, strengths and accomplishments for a purpose, and that purpose is to really make a difference in the community in which you live."

After the Oklahoma City bombing, Murali traveled back to Rajam, where he had established his first practice. G.M. Rao, a longtime friend and successful businessman, extended an invitation to host a party in Murali's honor. People in India had seen and read about his role in the Oklahoma City bombing, and there was great pride among his native friends and family. Murali and Sam were surprised that what they thought would be a small gathering was actually a celebration with more than 800 people. Friends, family and former patients showed up to celebrate and honor the local doctor who had made an impact in a faraway city in Oklahoma.

One man approached Murali with his sick granddaughter.

At left, The State Capitol Building in Oklahoma City. (Photo used with permission, The Oklahoman.)

She was suffering from polio. Murali explained to the gentleman that he no longer practiced general medicine, but the man had unwavering faith in him because he had once saved his life many years ago. Murali could see the pain in the grandfather's eyes, but he knew he was unable to make a difference for the child. Murali was saddened to see that the man had nowhere to turn.

So many people suffer while searching for answers.

Whether in India or Oklahoma City, too many people go without help, without continuity of care. They bounce from emergency room to emergency room with no aftercare.

The wheels started to turn.

When Murali was elected president of the Oklahoma County Medical Society, he knew what he wanted to accomplish. He had a new platform from which to speak. He knew he could use that platform for good.

He knew too many Oklahomans were going to bed hurting.

"I knew they didn't know where to go to fix their hurt."

But while Oklahomans were hurting, he saw doctors all around him traveling to third-world countries to volunteer.

"They faced difficulties in travel, primitive conditions, mosquitoes, disease. They travel so far. They are giving something and expecting nothing in return but the joy in their patients' faces. They get hugs and flowers. It is a spiritual experience. They come back recharged. It is divine work."

Murali understood the joy the doctors experienced. He and Sam traveled to India each year to volunteer and help out in any way they could.

But there was a still number stuck in his mind.

It haunted him.

Twenty percent. One in five.

That's how many people were hurting in Oklahoma. That's

how many uninsured Oklahomans went to bed at night with little or no help. Sure, they could wait for hours in an emergency room, but that brought no continuity of care and no follow-up doctor visit. Something had to be done.

Murali asked doctors why they traveled around the world, but failed to help out in their own hometown.

The answer was glaring.

Lawsuits.

Doctors here could not afford to do volunteer work and risk getting sued.

"I asked them, 'If I could wave a wand and make the liability go away, would you care for these uninsured patients?' They said, 'Oh, heavens, yes.'"

Murali knew very little about the legislative process. But he deeply understood the need to remove barriers for doctors who wanted to help. He also knew that volunteering was not something that could be put off until retirement. He once knew a doctor who suffered an accident and was unable to continue in his practice.

"His biggest regret is that he would never be able to do the volunteer work he had always planned to do when he retired. Some people realize early they want to live life beyond their own needs. Lucky are those people who realize that fact. That's why they live every minute, every second."

Murali set out on a path to connect doctors with those in need.

Where to begin?

Oftentimes in life, like-minded people find one another. Paths intersect. Passions connect.

Sue Hale, Pam Troup and Jackie Jones were working with Central Oklahoma Turning Point, a major health initiative to improve the overall health of Oklahomans. National polls showed the state at the bottom of the list for a myriad of health indicators. The group set out to make a difference.

And that is when the passions collided.

Murali and Jana Timberlake, executive director of the Oklahoma County Medical Society, met with Sue and Pam. They determined they needed a summit to address the issues of the uninsured. Against all odds, it happened. Eleven hospitals were represented at the summit with top administrators sitting shoulder to shoulder.

The meeting lasted several hours. At the conclusion, all were in agreement to form an ad hoc committee to further study the problems facing the uninsured. Jon Lowry was the statistician who gathered anonymous data from all the emergency rooms, which was where uninsured patients turned when they were sick. The yearlong study revealed eye-opening facts. Ultimately the Health Alliance for the Uninsured was formed, and Pam Cross was hired as executive director.

But the highest hill was yet to be climbed.

The ever-looming threat of legal action still created fear among doctors and all the other healthcare providers.

Again, paths cross. This time, it was Senator Susan Paddack and Representative Doug Cox. They agreed to help Murali and his cohorts navigate the legislature to try and pass a bill in 2007 that would protect health care workers from litigation resulting from volunteerism.

Senate Bill 930.

Murali was ill-prepared for politics.

"I just knew I had a passion. As human beings, we all have an inner deep longing to connect and help others. If we can uncover it, it will come out. I've yet to see it fail. It is inherent in each of us."

Murali knew he could convince the legislators if they would

listen.

So he set out every Wednesday to talk with them face to face at the capitol.

He and Jana walked the halls week after week.

It paid off. The bill passed 99 to 1. And it was off to the governor's desk.

Then the phone call came.

Oklahoma Governor Brad Henry was going to veto the bill.

Murali was heartbroken.

Coincidentally, he was scheduled to speak to a group of civic leaders the next morning. Stan Hupfeld had asked him to stand in for him.

"I had the podium and I was going to use it for good. I pleaded with them to help. To use whatever influence they had to persuade the governor not to veto this very important legislation.

"After the meeting, I saw Tom Price, a senior executive with Chesapeake Energy, out in the hall. He immediately flipped open his phone and called the governor's office."

The next day at a friend's wedding, another person close to the governor also agreed to try and reach out to him.

And Central Oklahoma Turning Point stepped up to the plate en masse and sent faxes to the governor in support of the bill.

Murali doesn't know which effort changed the governor's mind or if it was a combination of all, but Senate Bill 930 was not vetoed. It became law.

There were no hard feelings between Gov. Henry and Murali. The governor later called him and asked him to serve on the State's Board of Health.

Today, more than 100 doctors volunteer their time to care for the uninsured. Hupfeld, Bruce Lawrence and the INTEGRIS family along with Di Smalley at Mercy Health Center continue to support and nourish the program.

Nurses, pharmacists, dentists and other health professionals across Oklahoma County also give freely to those less fortunate. Medical students donate hours and hours to the cause.

One medical student is honored annually with the R. Murali Krishna Award for Outstanding Community Service.

I have seen evidence of the Divine presence.
I want my family and future family to know that.
It is not as if He came and sat down beside me;
yet it is that clear to me.

CHAPTER TWENTY

DR. R. MURALI KRISHNA
ON LIFE AND LESSONS LEARNED

Namasthe.

Murali places his hands palm to palm. They are centered over his chest, level with his heart. He smiles slowly.

"Namasthe. My spirit to your spirit."

The Indian doctor is more likely to give you a big hug than offer this ancient greeting, but the sentiment is just as strong.

"You are centering yourself, acknowledging your own spirit and offering it to another. It is all about connecting."

Connecting with one another and connecting with the Creator.

It's one of the many lessons Dr. R. Murali Krishna would like to pass on to his grandchildren and their children.

TRUST IN GOD

"I have seen evidence of the Divine presence. I want my family and future family to know that. It is not as if He came and sat down beside me; yet it is that clear to me.

"You have to look for it."

Future generations should learn the lessons he learned from Thatha.

"Look for the good in people. We are more than skin and bones. There is a definite presence of something extremely powerful, extremely loving and extremely healing. But you must go through your own journey to discover its fullness."

He knows his family will not be shielded from suffering, but he wants them to know they can trust in God.

"Don't let the immediacy of a situation dominate your actions. One may not always realize the meaning of suffering. But over time you will gain clarity and understanding. It happened to me even though it was over a long period of time. Trust in God. Sign off every night knowing that He is in control."

BE GRATEFUL AND GIVE FREELY

"All the gifts – mental, physical, material and spiritual – given to you by the Creator are possessed by us for a very temporary time. They are gifts meant to be given away. What good is a gift if you do not use it for good? Be grateful for your gifts and use them to make a difference in the world."

He hopes future generations will have a strong sense of gratitude.

"Everything we possess is fleeting, even your gifts. Don't delay giving back. Everything is given to us for only a short period of time. Connect and be part of your community. Do what you can do to nurture your community. Don't get preoccupied with recognition. Do it because you want to do it. There is no better satisfaction than know that through your energy and your determination, you have helped create something. Know that part of your purpose is to leave the world a little bit better. In that, you will receive the ultimate recognition from God."

BE PRESENT; BE A WITNESS

Murali wishes patience and calm for generations to come.

"As you grow through the years, you will begin to see things differently. I want you to slow down and savor every moment. Look for the beauty around you and in those you come across. And don't carry hard feelings with you. Forgive. Let go of anger so it won't destroy you.

"If you need to make a change in your life, make it. If you can't, try to reframe the negative situation. Work at developing a new attitude."

Murali knows the power of the mind. He knows each of us is filled with intelligence — intelligence that we barely begin to use to its capacity. It is not what happens in our lives, but rather how we react.

"You don't have to have all the answers. So many things are out of our control. The one thing that is in our control is how we view what is happening. How we perceive it, process it and react to it is within our control. Step back and be an objective witness to what is unfolding. Picture yourself as if you were seated in an audience watching a drama unfold on a stage. Be present. Don't judge yourself. Stay off the roller coaster. Be a witness. The more you can be a witness to what is happening, the more joyful your life can be.

"That is what life is meant to be."

The basis of being a witness to your own life is **mindfulness.**

"If you detach and practice being a witness during happy times, you will better be able to detach in stressful situations. It can greatly enhance your life."

Through his many years of talking to patients, Murali fully grasps that we are more than the sum of our parts.

"You are not your sensations. You are not your thoughts. You are more than your thoughts and sensations. If you could go to a store and buy all the elements that make up the human body, put them in your hand and shake them – you would never develop a human being. At the center of all of us is our spirit.

"That is the real you."

DREAM BIG

"Anything is possible. I want future generations to fully embrace big dreams. If you put your mind to it and work hard for it, anything is truly possible. Be realistic as to the amount of energy it takes but know that you can follow your heart and make things happen.

"With the right mindset and attitude and willingness to share your insights, you have significant influence over other people. You can impact others in a positive way. It is not about controlling others, but using the gifts you were given to lead and motivate.

"I have been blessed with gifts in my life. I have turned tragedy to triumph. I made a deliberate choice to heal, be whole and live vibrantly. I will continue to fight to raise the level of awareness of diseases of the brain. And most of all...

"Please God, use me up before you take me."

ABOUT THE AUTHOR

R. Murali Krishna, MD, DLFAPA is co-founder and
president of the James L. Hall, Jr. Center for Mind, Body
and Spirit, an educational organization devoted to improving
health through raising awareness of the healing power of
the connection between mind, body, and spirit. He is also
president and chief operating officer of INTEGRIS Mental
Health, provider of adult and child/adolescent mental health
services including inpatient, residential, outpatient &
clinical settings; an employee assistance program, and crisis
intervention services.

Along with Dr. Krishna's roles at James L. Hall, Jr. Center
for Mind, Body and Spirit and INTEGRIS Mental Health, he
serves on many professional and civic boards and committees.
He currently serves as president of the Oklahoma State Board
of Heath and is the founding president/president emeritus of
the Health Alliance for the Uninsured (HAU), a partnership
to improve the health care of the uninsured and underinsured
in Oklahoma County. He was the catalyst for getting key
legislation that gives protection for all health professionals
when they volunteer to help the poor and uninsured.

He is a Clinical Professor of Psychiatry at the University of
Oklahoma Health Sciences Center, Department of Psychiatry
and Behavioral Sciences; Distinguished Life Fellow of the
American Psychiatric Association (DLFAPA), and Diplomat,
American Board of Psychiatry. He is an active member of
the American Medical Association, American Psychiatric
Association, Central Oklahoma Turning Point, Oklahoma

County Medical Society (past president), Oklahoma Psychiatric Physicians Association (past president), Oklahoma State Medical Association, Oklahoma Improvement Plan on Obesity Work Group, Oklahoma Health Improvement Plan/Children's Health Flagship Workgroup, Oklahoma City-County Health Department Wellness Now Executive Committee, Oklahoma State Department of Mental Health and Substance Abuse Work Group and other state and local wellness initiatives.

Dr. Krishna is committed to improving the health of the people in our community. He believes that each one of us has a responsibility to care for those in need and is grateful for the opportunity to create lasting positive changes in people's lives. He is an expert on emotional wellness and the mind, body and spirit connection and how each one influences the other. His tireless efforts to help those in need have earned him numerous national and international awards and recognitions including the Exemplary Psychiatrist Award from the National Alliance on Mental Illness; the Outstanding Asian American Award for his efforts to help the victims of the Oklahoma City bombing; the American Heart Association's Heart & Soul Appreciation Award; Distinguished Friend of National Alliance on Mental Illness (NAMI) Oklahoma Award in recognition of his outstanding leadership on behalf of persons with severe mental illness. In 2010 he was selected honorary chair of the 2010 NAMIWalk Changing Minds...One Step at a Time and co-chair in 2011. Dr. Krishna and his family established the "Dr. R. Murali Krishna Family Eliminate the Stigma" Award in 2010 as a way to annually honor persons or organizations that have shown an outstanding contribution to the community by eliminating the stigma about mental illness and improving the lives of those affected by mental illness. Dr. Krishna received the notable Oklahoma State Medical Association's Gordon

Deckert, MD Award for Outstanding Community Services during their annual meeting held in Tulsa, OK in 2008. The Award recognizes physicians for reaching Oklahomans through actions and activities that improve the overall health and well being of our citizens and have demonstrated a positive impact on both physicians and the patients they serve. On February 26, 2011 the first R. Murali Krishna, M.D. Award was given to a fourth year medical student at the OU College of Medicine. The Health Alliance for the Uninsured (HAU) and OU School of Medicine initiated the annual award as a way of recognizing Dr. Krishna for his years of dedication and service to HAU and its mission. On January 27, 2012, Dr. Krishna received the prestigious United Way John Rex Community Builder Award for his commitment and determination to find long-term solutions to community needs. At the Oklahoma State Medical Association Annual Meeting on February 28, 2012, Dr. Krishna received the very prestigious 2012 Ed Calhoon, MD, Leadership in Organized Medicine Award in recognition of his distinguished leadership and service to organized medicine at the county, state, and national levels. Dr. Krishna received the Champion of Change Award for his dedication to make a difference in the lives of those affected by mental illness at the National Alliance on Mental Illness (NAMI) luncheon, held in Oklahoma City on October 12, 2012.

Dr. Krishna is an inspiring and engaging speaker on mental health and mind, body, spirit medicine topics and is often interviewed by television and print news organizations for his expert opinion on mental and emotional health issues. He has been featured on network television news programs and publishes a column, Mind Matters™.

Learn more about living vibrant with podcast and other offerings at **drkrishna.com**